A FIELDBOOK FOR COMMUNITY COLLEGE

ONLINE INSTRUCTORS

A FIELDBOOK FOR COMMUNITY COLLEGE

ONLINE INSTRUCTORS

—— KENT FARNSWORTH AND TERESA BRAWNER BEVIS ——

Community College Press®

A division of the

American Association of Community Colleges

Washington, DC

The American Association of Community Colleges (AACC) is the primary advocacy organization for the nation's community colleges. The association represents more than 1,100 two-year, associate degree–granting institutions and more than 11 million students. AACC promotes community colleges through six strategic action areas: national and international recognition and advocacy, learning and accountability, leadership development, economic and workforce development, connectedness across AACC membership, and international and intercultural education. Information about AACC and community colleges may be found at www.aacc.nche.edu.

Design: McGaughy Design
Editor: Deanna D'Errico
Printer: Graphic Communications, Inc.

© 2006 American Association of Community Colleges

Community College Press
American Association of Community Colleges
One Dupont Circle, NW
Suite 410
Washington, DC 20036

Printed in the United States of America.

Library of Congress Cataloging-in-Publication Data

Farnsworth, Kent Allen.
    A fieldbook for community college online instructors / Kent Farnsworth, Teresa Brawner Bevis.
        p. cm.
    "A comprehensive guide to everything an online instructor needs to know—from designing a course, to using
    technology, to assessing students"—Provided by publisher.
    Includes bibliographical references and index.
    ISBN 978-0-87117-376-8
    1. Distance education. 2. Teaching—Computer network resources. 3. Computer-assisted instruction.
    4. College teachers—Inservice training. I. Bevis, Teresa Brawner. II. Title.
LC5800.F37 2006
378.1'734—dc22

                                                                                            2006100682

Contents

Introduction 1
   Purpose of This Book..............................1
   Brief Chapter Review.............................2

1 A Brief History of Distance Education 5
   The First Distance Educators...................5
   Twentieth-Century Expansion.................7
   An Age of Inventions............................7
   The Space Age....................................8
   Computers Everywhere 9

2 Distance Education Now 11
   Today's Plugged-In World 11
   Critics of Online Learning 12
   Advantages of Online Instruction 12
   The Quality Issue................................13
   Online Education and Social Reality........13
   Online as Enhanced Education...............13
   Is Teaching Online for You? 14

3 The Community College Student 15
   Student Profile 15
   Developmental Students 16
   Students at Risk...................................16
   Working With the Underprepared 17
   Students and Work 17
   Minimizing Risk 18
   Community College Students as Online Learners ...19
   Early Personal Contact 20
   The Millennials 21

4 Online Orientation 23
   Orientation Elements 23

   Orientation Examples 24
   Developing an Orientation 26
   Removing the Fear..............................27

**5 Who Should Teach Online—
and Who Shouldn't** 29
   Characteristics of Capable Teachers 29
   Online Readiness Checklist....................31
   Who Should Not Teach Online? 32
   Who Can Be More Effective Online?........32
   Finding Online Faculty 33
   Instructor Orientation..........................33
   Faculty Support Groups 34

6 Laying the Groundwork 35
   Course Size..35
   The Precourse Letter............................36
   Course Design....................................37
   Syllabus...38
   Course Subdivisions 38
   Using Seminars 39

7 Managing Your Course and Time 41
   Making the Best Use of Announcements.................41
   Course Information..............................43
   Course Documents..............................43
   Agendas 43
   Incorporating Learning Principles 44
   Using Lecture as a Learning Catalyst........46
   Building Learning Community
      Through Assignments 47
   Posting and Exchanging Documents........48
   Calendar 49

Creating a Grade Book................................49
Other Tools 50
Course Options...51

8 Facilitating Discussion and
Collaborative Exercises 53
Threaded Discussion 53
Framing Questions.....................................56
Collaborative Exercises..............................58

9 Bells and Whistles 63
Enhanced Graphics....................................63
Animation 65
Photos..65
Audio 68
Video 69
Hypertext Markup Language (HTML) 71
Webcams 72
Bells and Whistles Without Technology....72

10 Getting Acquainted With Platforms....75
Primary Platforms 75
Course Development Providers...................76
Open-Source Course Management Systems.............76

11 In Loco Parentis Online 79
From the Instructor's Perspective..............80
First and Foremost, Know Who Your
Students Are...83
Meeting Your Students in Person 83
Fostering Responsible Students.................84

12 Encouraging Independent Work and
Addressing Academic Dishonesty 87
Strategies for Detecting and Preventing Academic
Dishonesty..87
Strategies for Encouraging Individual Work 88
Test Proctoring Strategies..........................88
Tailoring Assessment for Online Students...............89

Instructor Millie King Suspects
Academic Dishonesty 91
How Millie Addressed the Problem..........92
Typical Responses From Students Confronted
With Academic Dishonesty...................93
How Millie Resolved the Problem 94

13 Knowing the Law and Following It 97
What Is Copyrighted and What Is Not?....97
What Is Fair Use?.......................................98
Assorted Myths About Copyright Law.................100
Are There Exemptions for Online Instructors? 101
Performance Rights 101
What Is Ownership as It Pertains to Students
and Instructors? 102
Accessibility Issues 102
Family Educational Rights and Privacy Act............103
Slander...104

14 Hybrids and Learning Communities 105
Hybrid Classes 105
Course Management System Access........................106
A Hybrid Model.......................................108
Using Online Strategies to Build Learning
Communities 108

Conclusion 111

References 115

Glossary 119

Appendixes 123
A. Sample Materials for Online Instructors..........123
B. Quality Indicators for Community College
Online Programs 145

Index 151

About The Authors 167

Introduction

In community college academic and administrative meetings across the country, the same debate has raised tempers and created opposing camps for more than a decade: What do we do about online education? Its detractors question its merit relating to academic quality, student engagement, and faculty load, yet its supporters tout its value for recruiting teachers and students, innovating, and improving student involvement and—yes—instructional quality! Each side can point to a growing body of literature that it views as supporting its position, and either can poke holes in the other's research base.

Purpose of This Book

We begin this book by asserting that, like it or not, online instruction is rapidly gaining momentum as a critically important instructional methodology for community colleges. We assume also that both the debate and the research that fuels the debate will continue and that we will learn more each year about what works and does not work in distance education. The authors are two enthusiastic and committed online teachers who believe that this form of distance learning not only is effective but also addresses some common learning challenges in ways that are more successful than the traditional classroom approach. It is a book for those who are willing to entertain the thought that online instruction can be a dynamic and powerful teaching methodology, either as stand-alone delivery or in hybrid form, and who aspire to use the process to its fullest benefit.

At the same time, we have made every attempt to be objective about online instruction's assets and liabilities. It is not right for every student, nor can

every faculty member be an effective Web-based instructor. The technology involved assumes a certain set of interests and skills; these skills are discussed frankly and in some depth. There are a number of other books out there about online instruction. But we are writing specifically for those instructors working in the community college sector, where there are specific student-related issues that must be considered if online instruction is to be successful. How, for example, will underprepared students respond to an online environment? Can the technology and the needs of those who will have to use it accommodate developmental education, or should online instruction be limited to college-level course work? How well does online instruction work for students with broadly divergent ages, backgrounds, preparation, and interests—the students who typically attend community colleges? Is it reasonable to use online instruction as the only delivery method for critical or required portions of a curriculum or program?

We address each of these questions within the context of a systematic presentation that includes a brief history, a review of the current state of the methodology, and a discussion of community college students' characteristics. We then review course design with these characteristics in mind and offer techniques and applications that can energize students and produce exciting learning outcomes. The book is designed in such a way that in addition to being a readable primer, it can continue to serve as a reference and resource guide for online instruction. It provides an easy-to-follow table of contents, chapter subheadings that move you quickly and logically through the various information categories, and a useful glossary of terms to help you deal with the jargon of the discipline. It is a "read it through, then keep it close" resource for any online teacher—designed to be informative and practical.

Brief Chapter Review

In the first chapter, we present a brief history of distance education. You will see from this historical review that many of the basic issues routinely surfacing in faculty debates on the topic are not much different than they were when Caleb Phillipps began teaching shorthand by correspondence in the early 1700s. The history brings the reader up to date regarding the background of distance learning and illustrates the progression of delivery methods and sequences of events that led to the sophisticated Web-based systems used today.

Chapter 2 offers a review of the current state of online education, with specific attention given to the rationale for using online learning in community colleges. We provide an overview of the data concerning quality issues and comparative learning and discuss the advantages and disadvantages of this delivery method. We assert that online delivery provides some benefits that are difficult or impossible to provide in the on-ground classroom, such as asynchronous participation, distance access, required involvement, and immediate access to rich resources.

The nature of the community college online student is the subject of chapter 3. Here we review the general characteristics of community college students, with an explanation about why Web-based distance learning is ideally suited to many of them. We also examine how the format presents particular challenges for other students and suggest ways to address these challenges. We cite existing literature about how community college students respond to various instructional approaches and provide recommendations for maximizing effectiveness as an online teacher.

In chapter 4 we outline the need for and benefits of an effective online orientation to be offered as a prerequisite to initial enrollment in a Web-based course. This orientation aids students in determining the appropriateness of their equipment with regard to the requirements of the college's courses, how ably they can navigate in the online environment, and how the platform used by the college affects the process. An effective orientation addresses many of the basic questions about online courses and can save instructors hours of time.

Chapter 5 addresses who should teach online classes and who should not. We explain why online instruction ideally meets the teaching needs of many departments and instructors, allowing faculty to teach from campus, home, or a tropical beach. Web-based instruction allows colleges to extend their teaching base across the country and around the world, adding diversity and experience where it may not exist in the community. We also explain that online instruction may actually improve some teachers' effectiveness, but others will find that they are not suited to Web-based delivery. The chapter includes a brief checklist to assist the reader in determining his or her suitability to teach online and outlines the essentials of a good, basic orientation for online instructors.

Two of the most critical elements of an effective online course are getting information to students early about how the course works and designing a complete and useful syllabus. In chapter 6 we describe in detail how to contact students early with critical course information, how to prepare and use an effective syllabus, and how to begin to "calendar" the course so that students know what to expect and when. We describe the creation of agendas that break the course into learning units that include specific objectives, week-by-week assignments, due dates, and the like.

One of the common criticisms of online courses is that they require a lot more instruction time than an on-ground class. Although there is some truth to this criticism, instruction time can be greatly reduced through the use of successful course management strategies. In chapter 7 we discuss how to most effectively use the online format to maximize students' learning while managing instruction time. We encourage faculty who have taught for many years in a classroom to think of instruction differently, taking advantage of Web resources and resisting the temptation to simply import old traditional materials into the computer. We review techniques for delivering interesting online lectures, using student groups, and taking full advantage of the immediate links the Web provides and suggest techniques for keeping online instruction from becoming overly time-consuming. We outline the basic technological tools available to the instructor and review the pros and cons of each.

Because of their importance, class discussion and collaborative activities are described separately in chapter 8. One of the great advantages of online learning is that students can—and in most cases must—become involved in class discussion. Therefore, one of the most useful skills for instructors to have is the ability to manage and facilitate this dialogue effectively. We recommend a number of strategies for involving students in collaborative activities that support learning objectives.

Despite what some of the technophiles might want us to believe, an effective online learning environment can be created without all the bells and whistles. Still, a course that introduces some of the more sophisticated elements of Web-based technology can add interest and contribute to learning. In chapter 9 we discuss a number of the more sophisticated tools available to online instructors, such as streaming video, webcams, and imported or implanted video and audio files. We caution against creating class projects and requirements that exceed students' computer skills or equipment capabilities but explain how to access, create, or develop some of these more common tools if the instructor desires.

In chapter 10 we provide a brief overview of the most commonly used platforms and discuss the major differences between them. We then review in greater detail the newly developing open-source course management systems, such as Moodle and Sakai, that allow colleges to provide online instruction without the cost of the commercial platforms. We examine the compatibility between these open-source systems and com-

mercial platforms to help readers determine how easily they can be used to develop courses.

In chapter 11 we emphasize that online instructors must, in spite of physical distance and some degree of anonymity, interact with their students in personal and caring ways that may exceed traditional expectations. An online environment can be a surprisingly warm and welcoming place, with familiar faces and a hands-on instructor who serves as a leader, mentor, facilitator, and advocate for students. The ability of the instructor to display an element of personal interest in each student, as well as enthusiasm for the subject matter, requires strong interpersonal skills and intentional activity. We describe techniques for interjecting a sense of interest and enthusiasm into the course that aids students' performance and retention.

One of the often-expressed concerns about Web-based instruction is that it appears to lend itself to academic dishonesty. Preventing online cheating, identifying plagiarism, and assessment are the main topics in chapter 12. We suggest techniques for ensuring that students are doing their own work, for assessing students' work, and for using assessment as an additional learning tool. Common examples of academic dishonesty in online classes are provided from a cross-section of instructors, followed by explanations of how the problems were addressed and resolved.

In chapter 13 we examine legal issues related to copyright, fair use, and other proprietary rights questions. In this chapter, we discuss the instructors' responsibilities as they relate to protecting the rights of students, particularly concerning the Family Educational Rights and Privacy Act (FERPA), with illustrations of how the online environment creates confidentiality issues that may not be common in the on-ground classroom.

Many colleges are moving rapidly toward what are commonly called hybrid classes—courses that combine traditional classroom work with online supplements and activities. In chapter 14 we discuss hybrids and the value of Web-based instruction as part of the rapidly growing learning college movement. Hybrid courses are used to shorten time in the classroom by moving instruction into the Web environment or to add enrichment to the curriculum. Learning communities bring a cohort of students together in a combination of shared experiences, adding support to each student's learning. An online component can be used to both create and strengthen this community, even on an international basis, and can acquaint students with the world of computer-assisted learning while being surrounded by a strong support group. We also offer a look at the future of online instruction in community colleges and project issues and trends in Web-based learning in the new millennium. The chapter concludes with a rationale for the continuation and expansion of online learning in the community college curriculum and encourages today's faculty to grasp the opportunity to become pioneers in this exciting approach to learning.

Throughout this book we have scattered tips, received by e-mail, from some of the best online community college faculty we could identify. The tips cover teaching techniques, solutions to specific problems, uses of innovative technology, and advice on engaging students. In appendix A, we have included sample teaching materials. We hope that the tips and materials we have provided will help experienced and novice online instructors with good advice about how to make a Web-based course one of the highlights of a student's academic experience. Our expectation for the text is that, as we stated as the Introduction began, our readers will want to read it through, then keep it close.

A Brief History of Distance Education

The history of distance education dates from antiquity, and many of the issues that faced

its pioneers are still confronted today. In this chapter, we review the path distance learning

has taken and the events that have suddenly and dramatically elevated the field

to one of new and critical importance for community colleges.

Higher education is being pursued by an unprecedented number of increasingly nontraditional students. Just as the employment of children was the perpetuating force of the industrial age, the education of adults and universal access to information is the stimulus of our emerging information society (Holmberg, 1986). Community colleges, because of their accessibility, flexibility, ever-broadening areas of specialization, and comparatively low tuitions, are assuming greater levels of responsibility for meeting the educational expectations and obligations of the new millennium. The challenge for community colleges has been to provide increasing access to educational opportunities to an ever-expanding array of both traditional and nontraditional students, typically on a very constrained budget. One way community colleges are working to meet this challenge is by expanding their commitment to distance learning and online education in particular.

Offering courses that can be accessed from remote locations and that do not require classroom attendance is a highly efficient means of serving greater numbers of students, but it is certainly not a new idea. Evidence of distance learning can be traced back to the 18th century, when some schooling was reportedly conducted by exchange of letters. Since then, the history of distance education leading up to today's Web-based formats can be summarized within the following periods:

1700s–mid-1900s	Correspondence courses
1950s–1960s	Video conferencing
1950s–1980s	Teleconferencing
1990s–present	Web-based instruction

The First Distance Educators

Among the first attempts at distance education was the introduction of an innovative idea by Caleb Phillipps, an 18th-century American entrepreneur in Boston. Phillipps's idea focused on the notion that education could be successfully carried out through the exchange of a series of written documents, transferred between parties by local letter carriers and messenger services. Phillipps was convinced he could capitalize on the idea and developed a "correspondence" method of teaching his shorthand course. He organized the course into manageable increments that could be doled out to students in periodic doses over a period of several months and devised a means of assessing performance. On March 20, 1728, he purchased an advertisement in the *Boston Gazette* that read as follows:

> Caleb Phillipps, "Teacher of the New Method of Short Hand," advising that any "Persons in the Country desirous to Learn this Art, may by having the several Lessons sent weekly to them, be as perfectly instructed as those that live in Boston." (Holmberg, 1986, p. 6)

It is unclear how successful Phillipps's course was or exactly how many students he enrolled, but it appears to have been the first documented attempt at distance education. Almost a century later, Sir Isaac Pitman, another expert in shorthand, decided to try correspondence as a form of distance learning. In 1840, he began teaching his method by mail in Bath, England, fashioning his course to cater to adults who did not have time during the day to attend school.

Pitman's course required students to copy an assigned number of Biblical passages in shorthand onto small sheets of paper he had customized to resemble postcards. After completion of the assignment, students returned the postcards to him via the Penny Post. Pitman evaluated the assignments, determined whether the work was executed to his satisfaction, noted his responses on the cards, and mailed them back to his students. When the designated number of exchanges was complete, a closing letter was provided to the student that indicated his or her successful completion of the course (Holmberg, 1986).

A succession of similar efforts to educate people at a distance continued through the second half of the century on both sides of the Atlantic. In 1856, Frenchman Charles Toussaint and German Gustav Langenscheidt began a school in Berlin; they taught language courses in Europe by correspondence. Two years later, the University of London began its External Programme to make degrees accessible to students who, for one reason or another, could not come to the university to study in the conventional way (Holmberg, 1986).

Across the Atlantic in the United States, Anna Eliot Ticknor and William Rainey Harper were busy establishing The Society to Encourage Study at Home. Fully operational as early as 1873, this correspondence school created a structured method of exchanging commentary with students. The school included six departments—History, Science, Art, Literature, French, and German—and offered 24 subjects. Each course required monthly correspondence via the postal system between teachers and students, complete with guided readings and tests. The society at one time enrolled approximately 1,000 men and women and operated until Ticknor's death in 1897 (Verduin & Clark, 1991).

In 1874, Wesleyan University in Illinois started a distance program, offering both graduate and undergraduate degrees in absentia. This was the first university-level distance study in America. Seven years later, William Rainey Harper, drawing on his earlier experiences with correspondence education in Boston, further influenced distance education by initiating the Correspondence School of Hebrew. These early efforts, combined with his later initiatives in the field of distance education at the University of Chicago, have prompted many to refer to Harper as "the father of distance education" (Verduin & Clark, 1991, p. 7).

Near the end of the century, Cornell University also introduced a distance learning model by establishing a correspondence university based at its home campus. The correspondence university was founded in Ithaca, New York, by 32 university professors from a cross-section of colleges and universities (including Harvard, Johns Hopkins, and the University of Wisconsin). In 1883, Cornell's new Chautauqua Institute was authorized by New York to award degrees by correspondence. Students were required to successfully complete the academic work through workshops conducted entirely by mail.

The University of Wisconsin was the first American institution to propose correspondence study in its 1889–1890 catalog as a function of university extension. Two years later, the university coined the term *distance education* in its 1892 catalog. According to university archivists, this was the first time the term was used.

At about the same time, The Colliery Engineer School of Mines in Wilkes-Barre, Pennsylvania, began offering a home study course in mining through the efforts of Thomas J. Foster, an expert in mines and mine safety. The project became so critical to the institution's activities that The Colliery Engineer School of Mines eventually changed its name (and broadened its mission), becoming the International Correspondence Schools (Verduin & Clark, 1991). In 1892, Pennsylvania State College started offering correspondence courses in agricultural studies. At the same time, The University of Chicago, now under the dynamic leadership of William Rainey Harper, was also actively developing and promoting courses by mail.

Europe paralleled many of America's initiatives. In 1894, the Rustinches Fernlehrinstitut, created to help prepare students for university entrance examinations through correspondence, was established in Berlin. The same year, Diploma Correspondence College, now called Wolsey Hall, in Oxford, England, was founded to prepare students for university qualifications and offered a wide range of other subjects as well. Four years later (1898), Sweden's Hans S. Hermod initiated his namesake correspondence school as a result of trying to help a single student whose education was being neglected because he was unable to attend a traditional classroom. A few years later, Norwegian educator Ernst G. Mortensen traveled to Hermod's in Sweden to learn about the innovative school. After an enlightening visit that included interviews with some of Hermod's students, Mortensen returned to Norway to establish Norsk Korrespondanseskole, the first distance learning institution in that country (Verduin & Clark, 1991, p. 16).

Twentieth-Century Expansion

In the 20th century, distance education slowly expanded in scope, diversity, and enrollment, especially in the United States. Most of what was offered through distance learning was still highly specialized and catered to selected groups. For example, in 1900, Martha Van Rensselaer organized Cornell University's extension program in home economics specifically for New York State's rural women. In 1901, Moody Bible Institute began offering courses pertaining specifically to Christian philosophy through the Moody Correspondence School project. Four years later, the Calvert Day School began providing a curriculum by correspondence strictly for children of kindergarten age, and shortly thereafter The Federal Schools (which later changed its name to Art Instruction Schools) began advertising art courses by mail to aspiring artists (Watkins, 1991).

Distance education was clearly expanding in both course availability and enrollment, and many institutions of higher education took up the cause. By the early 20th century, any institution that was not yet participating in distance learning was at least taking significant notice of those that were. Charles Van Hise, the president of the University of Wisconsin during the first decade of the 20th century, announced the institution's renewed commitment to correspondence instruction after a period of some indifference. Van Hise, noting the success of several of the commercial correspondence schools, encouraged Wisconsin citizens to invest in their own system and took steps to create a division of correspondence study that included languages, literature, political economy, political science, history, sociology, mathematics, pure science and applied science (Watkins, 1991, p. 16).

An Age of Inventions

Until the end of the first decade of the 20th century, the town letter carrier served as the primary delivery system for distance learning. But new technologies such as the lantern slide and motion pictures were suddenly emerging, providing new and exciting visually based options for correspondence study. The first catalogs of instructional films appeared in 1910 and 1913. The renowned inventor Thomas Edison proclaimed his belief that the education system would be completely changed within a decade as a consequence of the invention of film (MacLean, 1925). Although Edison's prediction turned out to be premature, it was illustrative of the attention that many in both the public and private sectors were starting to give to the idea of distance education.

In addition to film, a promising new technology was emerging during the same period—instructional radio. From its inception, educational institutions were excited about the idea of offering information to their students over the airwaves and were eager to implement radio in the classroom. By the 1920s and 1930s, radio was being used extensively in educational settings.

The federal government granted more than 200 broadcasting licenses between 1918 and 1946 to educational institutions hoping to develop distance learning through instructional radio. Despite this initial enthusiasm by educators, the technology ultimately failed to attract a large audience; by 1940, few college-level courses were still being offered by radio transmission (Paulsen, 1992). Even as the use of radio declined in the 1930s, instructional television, the "new kid on the block," was being viewed with interest and optimism. In 1932, 7 years before television was introduced at the New York World's Fair, the State University of Iowa began experimenting with transmitting instructional courses via television. Soon fledgling efforts were being made by the academic mavericks of the day in institutions around the country. By the late 1930s, it was evident that the new visual distance learning technology was on the rise.

World War II slowed the introduction of television to the American public and curtailed its uses for education. It was during those years, however, that training efforts produced by the military clearly demonstrated the potential for using audiovisual media in almost any educational venue (Verduin & Clark, 1991, p. 17). As audiovisual media developed after the war, the potential for instruction outside the traditional classroom increased, with many colleges quickly incorporating the new technology.

This new interest in transferring knowledge from a distance through video also spawned related initiatives. For example, in 1952, the Joint Council on Educational Television, a group of professional educators, joined others in convincing the U.S. Federal Communications Commission (FCC) to reserve a segment of the television channel spectrum expressly for education, paving the way for the development of stations such as the Public Broadcasting System (Nasseh, 1997). As might be anticipated, this period of growth in distance learning provoked one repeated question among educators: Is it really comparable to on-site learning? Researchers were encouraged by early studies indicating that students learning via televised programming seemed to show the same levels of achievement as did those learning through face-to-face instruction. A study by Parsons in 1957 showed only borderline differences in achievement between the two methods, and another study by Lapore and Wilson (1958) a year later again produced similar results (see also Jeffries, 2001).

The Space Age

In July 1962, the United States launched its first communications satellite, Telstar I. Because it was in a low orbit, massive antennas were required, and continuous communication was impractical at first. But later satellites, placed in orbit at approximately 22,000 miles over the equator, enabled worldwide teleconferencing and two-way video contact for the first time in history.

Teleconferencing allowed colleges to select among a number of formats, with one-way video/ two-way audio proving the most common. However, two-way audio/two-way video quickly became more affordable, and telecourses became a common distance-learning format in the 1960s. During that period, several major telecourse development projects were funded by the Annenburg Foundation, the Corporation for Public Broadcasting, and a number of public universities and community colleges. The Carnegie Commission on Higher Education predicted that by the year 2000, more than 80% of off-campus and 10% to 20% of on-campus instruction would take place through telecommunications (Saettler, 1968, p. 68).

In the late 1960s and early 1970s, new microwave technology developed, and institutions of higher education began setting up microwave networks to take advantage of the Instructional Television Fixed Service authorized by the FCC. Within a decade, another boost to distance education occurred when cable and satellite television came into use, essentially expanding the reach of education through telecommunications throughout the world. The introduction in 1971 of the Open University in Great Britain created the world's first university to teach only at a distance, enrolling students worldwide. Indicative of the importance of the new media, the Open University was originally supposed to be called the University of the Air, but the name was abandoned for the more generic title.

Computers Everywhere

Although the incorporation of cable and satellite transmission in the 1970s and 1980s was critical to distance learning, nothing could compare with the transforming impact of the technology that was just on the horizon. The advent of the Internet and digital applications in the 1990s, combined with the changing demographics of the distance learner, at once added an entirely new and virtually limitless dimension to the field of distance education. This astonishing new technology instantly resulted in unprecedented educational opportunities for both traditional and nontraditional students, as well as the lure of increased enrollments for colleges and universities.

The "virtual classroom," which now allows students to fully participate wherever and whenever there is a computer, has had a monumental impact on the distance-learning format. Through the use of computer groupware, or more popularly, the Internet via the World Wide Web, students enroll in classes using a computer at home, at work, or somewhere on campus to access the course, rather than occupy a desk at a specific time. They register online, download course materials, gain access to video and audio resources, and communicate with both the instructor and other students in the class.

Various terms have been coined in recent years to describe this approach to learning: the virtual classroom, cyber-learning, e-learning, and so on. All describe the same thing and fall under the umbrella of distance or distributed education. For the purpose of continuity, in this book we use the generally familiar terms *online* or *Web-based* interchangeably to describe computer-generated, interactive course work within the field of distance education.

An online class can be formatted to be synchronous, asynchronous, or a combination of both. Synchronous communication occurs when the students and their instructor meet online in real time (at the same time) in a computer format such as a chat room to discuss topics, issues, and concerns surrounding the class. Asynchronous communication occurs via announcements, bulletins, discussion boards, and e-mail. Asynchronous information may be posted at any time and read by the intended recipient whenever convenient.

Online education is now rapidly and fundamentally changing the way colleges approach instruction as a whole. Distance learning by means of computer is a new way to expand education at minimal cost but with no apparent limit to an institution's reach. Community colleges have been especially aggressive in expanding their enrollments through online study. Their flexibility and their expertise in handling a multitude of educational tasks makes them the perfect venues for experimenting with new learning techniques, including online instruction. Aside from the readily apparent enrollment advantage of accessibility and convenience for students, community colleges also are reaping the benefit of being able to draw from a wider pool of qualified instructors. Many potential faculty who were previously excluded because they lived too far away from campus or were unable to teach in traditional places at traditional times are now able to offer their expertise.

The rapid expansion of online instruction in community colleges has been hampered, however, by one key component: preparation of faculty. In many cases adjunct instructors hired to teach online courses or existing faculty new to teaching online are offered little or no specialized guidance to prepare them for the unique challenges of the community college online environment. In addition, rarely do community colleges provide their online staff any information or training related to the historical foundations of the field. By providing a historical summary of the development of distance education, a thorough how-to overview of basic practices, and a collection of insiders' tricks of the trade, this book gives online instructors an understanding of the field that is practical, comprehensive, and balanced.

CHAPTER 2

Distance Education Now

In this chapter, we discuss the rationale for the use and expansion of online instruction in today's community colleges. We provide a review of the research concerning quality and delivery methodologies and introduce the reader to the advantages and disadvantages of online learning.

Virtually all of the distance education methods discussed in chapter 1 are still in use somewhere in higher education today. Interactive telecourses are mainstays of many distance education programs, although they are losing popularity to Web-based instruction and the accompanying webcam technologies now in use. Cable systems still make public access channels available for educational broadcasts using one-way video programming. Even the exchange of handwritten letters is used by faculty teaching business correspondence or interpersonal communication, helping students gain an appreciation for the personal touch provided by this practice. The focus of this book, however, is exclusively on Web-based or online course delivery, although some other methods may be mentioned on occasion, either in contrast or as they relate to this particular instructional delivery system.

Today's Plugged-In World

It is not surprising that with the explosive growth in personal computer ownership and Internet access during the last two decades, their use for educational delivery also has grown exponentially. According to the LexisNexis Statistical Web site (2005), the number of computers in use in the United States has closely mirrored the population, with 296 million people in the country in 2005 and 250 million computers in use. Projections are that in 2009, the ratio will be even closer to 1:1, with a population of 307 million and 292 million computers being used. The research suggests that by this time, nearly 250 million of these users will take advantage of the Internet—virtually everyone of school age or older—and nearly all of these users will be cellular phone subscribers (LexisNexis, 2005).

With this degree of home computer access, particularly among those with college-aged students, interest in distance education was destined to follow a similar growth curve. Analysts with International Data Corporation estimated that 5% of higher education students were involved in distance learning in the United States in 1998, with a projection of 15% by 2002 and compounded annual growth of 33% (Oblinger, Barone, & Hawkins, 2001). By 2004, more than 80% of campuses participating in an online survey administered by Campus Computing Project reported wireless networks on campus, making delivery of Web-based or electronically hybridized courses a relatively simple task, even for students receiving all of their course work on campus (Campus Computing Project, 2004).

This use of instructional delivery to students on campus, but not in the classroom, has led in recent years to the use of the label "distributed education" when referring to these methods, because they are not necessarily used by students at a distance. In the American Council on Education's first publication in a series titled "Distributed Education: Challenges, Choices, and a New Environment," the authors noted, "We prefer the term *distributed* learning over *distance* education because distance is too restrictive of a concept" (Oblinger et al., 2001, p. v). In this book we will occasionally use the terms interchangeably, but unless otherwise noted, we refer to online learning.

Critics of Online Learning

Despite the lessons described in chapter 1, this radically different approach to teaching and learning has not been universally embraced within the academic community. Just as they did in the 19th and 20th centuries, critics have raised questions about quality, learning effectiveness, academic integrity, and potential effects on academic culture. Many of the criticisms that are not focused on quality raise concerns that online education would result in less student-to-student and faculty-to-student interaction, leading to an experience devoid of inspirational moments (Moriber, 2000).

In an article in *Change,* Armstrong (2000) argued that a radical shift to distributed education would reduce the amount of mentoring and socialization that students receive within the academy and that students would lose this valued aspect of the postsecondary learning experience. Later, Carriuolo (2002) expressed many of the same concerns, especially as they relate to the kinds of students who frequent community colleges. Her sense was that first-generation students with a high need for socialization, significant academic support requirements, and limited technical expertise may not benefit from online learning in the same ways they might benefit from a campus-based experience.

These criticisms are not without merit, and it is not the purpose of this book to suggest that distance education is equivalent in every respect to a full-time campus experience. Yet these critics often idealize the campus experience by suggesting that most students regularly engage in serious discussion in class and enjoy casual conversation with peers or professors after hours. The 2004 findings of the Community College Survey of Student Engagement (CCSSE) revealed that this is anything but the case. In self-reported data, only 44% of students indicated that they often or very often worked together with other students during class. Only 21% reported that they worked with other students on projects outside of class. Sixty-three percent said they often or very often asked questions in class, meaning that more than a third did not, and only 15% indicated that they discussed ideas from readings or classes with instructors outside of class. Eighty-four percent said they never participated in college-sponsored activities (CCSSE, 2004).

Advantages of Online Instruction

Although we can present idealized accounts of students who regularly engage in stimulating discussion with peers outside of class, these students are clearly the exception in community colleges. In fact, the goal of online instruction should not be to duplicate the campus experience of the majority of community college students as it now exists but to dramatically improve on it. Teaching online is not simply a matter of moving the classroom onto the Web; it is an opportunity to explore learning in new ways—some only modestly new because of the medium and some radically so.

Research has shown that the mere process of reviewing class material, restructuring it for a new format, and delivering it differently may have positive value (Meyer, 2002). We might assume that this would be the case whenever a faculty member thoroughly reviews course content and considers new ways of presenting material. The opportunity that must be explored, though, is how online instruction, by nature of the medium and the tools afforded by technology, can actually produce better results than we typically find in the traditional classroom. For example, in later chapters we will illustrate how this teaching approach may serve to engage a greater number of students more effectively.

The Quality Issue

If the quality concerns raised by critics are merited, there may be reason to discourage participation in online instruction. However, this does not appear to be the case. The body of literature that compares learning outcomes for "on-ground" education to online learning is still spotty. Many of the studies are small and lack careful controls. However, to date there is little evidence to suggest significant differences in learning outcomes between online and classroom-based instruction.

Key questions in this debate focus on what constitutes learning and quality, and we could go on ad infinitum without reaching agreement. Current research does provide some insight, however. Meyer (2002), in a comprehensive review of the quality literature that had been published before 2002, cited Russell's review in 1999 of 355 studies on distance education. Russell concluded that whether courses were delivered in class or through any of the various distance-learning formats, there was no statistically significant difference in learning outcomes. Concerning instructional delivery, Russell stated, "No matter how it is produced, how it is delivered, whether or not it is interactive, low-tech or high-tech, students learn equally well" (cited in Meyer, 2002, p. 14). Meyer noted, however, that in several of these and later studies, some difference was found in student persistence and in satisfaction with the learning experience, both issues that will be discussed in later chapters.

Much of the research that has suggested "no significant difference" has been criticized as having been poorly designed, with questionable research methodology (Joy & Garcia, 2000; Moore & Thompson, 1997). But the fact remains that existing research generally supports the claim that there is no significant difference between how effectively students learn using online instruction and classroom-based delivery.

Online Education and Social Reality

In her article expressing concern about socialization and distributed learning, Carriuolo (2002) related a story told at a conference by one of the speakers. This unidentified presenter touched the audience with the account of a mountain woman, a single mother of four, who was able to complete a degree only because she could participate online. The speaker then incensed many of the women attending by stating that "This woman doesn't need to be on a college campus." The reaction of a woman in the audience was, "A college campus is exactly what she needs. Single with four children? She needs to learn a different way of life."

Whether an on-campus experience might have been more beneficial to this woman is incidental. She could not have availed herself of that opportunity. Residential attendance was simply beyond her circumstances and means. However, through online learning, she was able to improve the circumstances of herself and her family well beyond what would have been possible otherwise.

Distributed learning is a reality of today's educational world. It is with us now and will continue to be in one form or another. We can argue about whether we would like it to be otherwise—with all students attending small liberal arts colleges where they gather with faculty on the quad and ruminate over the lessons of the previous hour. Nevertheless, that will not change the reality. Roughly half of today's freshmen begin in community colleges, with a high percentage supporting families and working part or full time. It is our responsibility to ensure that we make the community college experience as meaningful as possible for those who complete part of that journey online.

Online as Enhanced Education

A good case can be made that some elements of learning are actually enhanced through online education. The obvious advantage, and one needing little elaboration, is that it can be delivered at a distance. The mountain woman can receive her degree, even if unable to leave her four children and come to a campus. She also can do it at times that accommodate her schedule. Online instruction can be completely asynchronous—meaning that she, other students in the class, and the instructor participate at different times as their schedules permit. A third benefit is that it can be delivered relatively inexpensively. All that is required of the student is access to a computer and an Internet connection, making a public library, community center, or Internet café a suitable classroom.

Other advantages are not quite as apparent. One relates to the surveyed students mentioned previously who had never engaged in discussion in class. Students in a well-designed and well-delivered Web-based class simply cannot be non-participants. Each must participate regularly and on an essentially equal basis with others. A second unique value is that the online environment places students within a mouse click of almost limitless resources. Imagine, for example, the value of being engaged in a discussion of Zoroastrianism in a world religions course and having a link to www. sacred-texts.com/index.htm. Here, 1,000 of the world's great religious works, including the Zoroastrian Avesta, are available to students in full translation. A teacher can, of course, have access to these links in a classroom equipped with a Smart Board or computer projector. But even if they are in a classroom with this technology, faculty can rarely afford the time to allow students to surf the site, explore other titles, and become immersed in the world of sacred literature.

Students also find that they are much more thoughtful about responses when posting them to a discussion board where they will be carefully read by the teacher and classmates. The loss of spontaneous discussion is often cited as a disadvantage of asynchronous learning. However, it is easily compensated for by the quality of dialogue that develops as students thoughtfully consider how to respond to a teacher's questions or the comments of others.

Opportunity for thoughtful preparation manifests itself in a number of other ways in online courses. In a conversation between an online speech teacher and several on-ground colleagues, one colleague expressed concern about the online teacher's reliance on taped speeches. "I think it critical that my students speak before an audience," she said. "I have my students tape their speeches in front of an audience." Without thinking, one of the other colleagues retorted, "But they could practice the speech a dozen times before taping the final version!" The online instructor was quick to point out that this kind of practice would be a speech teacher's dream.

A less course-specific value of online learning is that it contributes to an emerging educational imperative: technological literacy. A well-designed and appropriately structured Web-based course can advance even technological novices to the point where they can comfortably exchange information using e-mail, attachments, drop boxes, and chat rooms. They also can access library resources online and navigate other Web sites with relative ease. Yet it is still quite possible for a student to emerge from a full semester in a traditional classroom with no added technological knowledge.

Is Teaching Online for You?

Not every faculty member will make a great online teacher, any more than every faculty member makes a great teacher in other settings. Great online teaching requires a willingness to develop relationships through written language, paying particular attention to meaning as it is relayed by word rather than gesture. The attributes of excellent online teaching will be discussed in detail in chapter 5. However, it is important to note that effective Web-based instruction requires dedication, imagination, and commitment to every student. Teachers will interact with each student in ways that rarely happen in the on-ground class.

Nor does every student make a capable online learner. In the next chapter, the characteristics of community college students are reviewed, with discussion of those attributes that contribute to or distract from effective online learning.

CHAPTER 3

The Community College Student

In this chapter, we review the characteristics of community college students and explain why Web-based distance learning is ideally suited to many of them. We also examine how the format presents particular challenges for many students and suggest ways to address these challenges.

Students in the community college sector of higher education cover the full spectrum of characteristics and abilities. They range in age from late teens to octogenarians. In recent years, higher numbers of high school graduates have enrolled in community colleges because of low tuition, program interest, and convenience. As a result, the average student age has declined in many colleges, yet, nationally, it is still around 29. Educational backgrounds include home schooling, high school equivalency (general equivalency degree or GED), traditional high school graduation, and reverse transfer, whereby students with advanced degrees return to community colleges seeking special credentialing.

Student Profile

In their popular text, *The American Community College*, Cohen and Brawer (2003) provided a comprehensive statistical profile of students in this sector. They described them with a mean age of 29, a median age of 23, and a modal age of 19. In other words, although the average age is in the mid- to high 20s, the largest group continues to be the traditional student, recently out of high school. The significant number of older students—some considerably older—raise the mean to 29.

Approximately two thirds of community college students are part-time students, 58% are women, 66% are enrolled seeking a degree or certificate of some kind, and 21% enroll to improve job skills. Minority students are more likely to attend community colleges than 4-year institutions. Of this group, 47% of African Americans, 56% of Hispanics, and 57% of Native Americans are enrolled in this sector (Phillippe & González-Sullivan, 2005). Twenty-eight percent of community college students come from the bottom quartile of the socioeconomic spectrum, whereas 19% fall in the top quartile. These figures are virtually reversed in the 4-year sector, where 27% are in the top quartile and 19% are in the bottom (Cohen & Brawer, 2003). Although 65% of 4-year students work while in school, 81% of community college students are employed and on average work twice as many hours as those enrolled in 4-year institutions (American Council on Education, 2003).

Developmental Students

It is difficult to say exactly what percentage of community college students require developmental academic assistance, because this is neither uniformly tested nor reported. The National Center for Educational Statistics (NCES) longitudinal study of students entering higher education in 1995–1996 reported that 41% of students in the 2-year cohort required at least one developmental course (Lewis & Farris, 1995). But in recent years, other leaders in higher education have placed the number at more than 50% (Paredes, 2005). The most recent report issued by the Achieving the Dream: Community Colleges Count initiative, funded by the Lumina Foundation, indicated that approximately 80% of the students in the 2002 cohort (approximately 27 colleges) were referred to developmental education in at least one subject (Clery & Solórzano, 2006). Whatever the number, it can safely be said that a significant percentage of community college students require developmental assistance in reading, mathematics, or English.

Teaching Tip

Try a mix-and-match approach to course materials and divide the workload into information and interaction segments. Design the information segments to appeal to different learning styles; consider slide presentations, mini lectures, video tutorials, and resource links. Add a weekly discussion pulled from the information segment and encourage students to use examples from their own experiences in their responses.

—Susan Holmes
online communications instructor
NorthWest Arkansas Community College

Students at Risk

These data are little more than statistics until examined in light of their potential implications for students in our classrooms. The NCES study mentioned previously cited a 1992–1993 national finan-cial aid survey that identified seven factors correlated with the likelihood that students will not succeed in college (Lewis & Farris, 1995):

- Not enrolling in postsecondary education within the same year as graduating from high school
- Attending school part time
- Being financially independent of parents
- Working full time
- Having dependents other than a spouse
- Being a single parent
- Not having received a standard high school diploma

Other studies have shown that high financial need, even if met with considerable financial aid, is a critical risk factor. An internal assessment conducted by Mountain Empire Community College in Virginia, where 93% of students in the sample year completed a student financial aid application, revealed that the degree of financial need correlated directly with risk of dropping out (Mountain Empire Community College, 2006). Enrollment in developmental courses is also a significant risk factor, and the greater the number of developmental courses a student takes, the greater the degree of risk (Hoyt, 1999). Given these risk indicators, consider this description of first-time community college students provided by the NCES report (Lewis & Farris, 1995):

1. Approximately one third of these first-time students were financially independent.
2. Of the two fifths who took a standardized admission test, 43% scored in the lowest quartile of all beginning postsecondary students who took a test, and only 10% scored in the highest quartile.
3. Approximately 40% received some form of financial aid, 8% obtained loans, and 35% received grants or scholarships.
4. Approximately half (52%) had parents whose highest level of education was a high school diploma or less.
5. Nearly half (48%) delayed entering a postsec-

ondary institution for at least 1 year.

6. Almost half (46%) enrolled part time.

7. Approximately one fifth did not work while enrolled; fewer than 10% worked an average of 1–15 hours per week. However, approximately one third (35%) worked full time (35 hours or more).

Using the seven factors listed, the authors of the NCES study created four risk categories. They noted that among those who enrolled as first-time attendees in community colleges in the 1995–1996 year,

- 25.7% showed no risk factors (compared with 69.6% in the 4-year sector).
- Slightly more than 22% had one risk factor.
- 28.1% were at moderate risk with two to three factors.
- 23.9% were at high risk with four or more factors.

In other words, more than half of this community college cohort was at moderate to high risk. This student profile presents daunting challenges to faculty under any circumstances—challenges that become even more pronounced when instruction is delivered online.

Perhaps the most underremediated learning deficiency for newly entering students is reading ability. Reading is assessed in many cases, but without mandatory placement in a developmental course, if called for. Faculty often oppose mandated reading placement, fearing that requiring it will significantly limit enrollment in their programs. Although more community colleges are mandating reading placement each year, the majority still do not. Therefore, online instructors easily may have a number of students in a reading-intensive course who have unremediated needs in this critical learning skill.

Working With the Underprepared

Cross (1999), citing Perry's work on stages of intellectual development, noted that students in the lower stages of development expect and require much more structured learning. They have a lower tolerance for ambiguity and expect authority figures to "have the answers" to academic questions. Students in more advanced stages of intellectual development are more inclined to question and to be more engaged in self-directed learning. Faculty teaching student groups with a significant mix in intellectual maturity face the challenge of balancing structured learning situations for the less mature with opportunities that stretch and satisfy the intellectually curious.

Students and Work

In a study of factors influencing persistence of adult learners, Kemp (2002) found that work commitments had a particularly detrimental effect on students' success. A series of what she called "resiliency skills" (ability to handle relationships effectively, initiative, personal resilience in the face of adversity, and insight) were especially helpful. Unfortunately, many of the students in online community college classes are working full or part time and are weak in a number of the resiliency skills mentioned by Kemp.

Yet, in several ways the online teaching format can accommodate this diverse set of learners more easily and more effectively than can the traditional classroom setting. At its best, it is "individualized group learning." If properly accommodated, courses that allow students to study and join in class at any time or place are ideally suited to those who attend part time, have heavy workloads, or have other significant out-of-school responsibilities. In addition, in the online environment, the instructor has an opportunity to discuss the personal learning experiences of each student in a private, unhurried setting.

Being able to accommodate these students where they are and when they can study may be the most critical factor in making higher education available. Knowing in advance about the 40-hour workload of a 19-year-old female student or the recent job loss of an older man can lay the groundwork for the right comment at the right time, the right twist on an assignment, and the right suggestion for a paper that can mitigate for many of these risk factors.

Minimizing Risk

Faculty will be inclined to say, "These strategies would be helpful in any class," and unquestionably they would be right. But it is a rare teacher who takes the time to get to know students that well. In the online environment, this familiarity can be a relatively simple process.

Every online delivery platform has a discussion area—a forum for creating what is called "threaded discussion." An essential first assignment for every Web-based class should be the posting of a brief personal biography by each student. (We will describe this again in the section on doing the groundwork in chapter 6.) Many faculty begin their traditional classroom sessions with a quick introductory icebreaker: Give us your name, tell us where you are from, and tell us something about yourself and why you have taken this class. The responses are generally perfunctory, with the exception of the half dozen students who see this as an opportunity to talk about themselves at length. In the online format, you as the teacher can structure the responses with a series of short questions and use follow-up questioning to learn additional information about students that will be helpful in improving the learning experience for each. Here is an example of a bio assignment that might assist with both creating a more comfortable social climate in the course, and with providing useful learning assistance:

For your first assignment, due Wednesday by 5:00 pm, provide a brief personal biography in the forum titled "Biographies" on the discussion board. Because many of us will not be meeting in person, tell us something about yourself that will help us "know you." For example

- How would you briefly describe yourself in a letter to someone you have never met?
- What would you like us to know about your family and how you spend most of your time? Are you working while going to school? Are you a full-time student?
- How would you like to be spending most of your time?

- What about this class are you particularly looking forward to or worrying about?
- What one or two things about you will help us know you best as an online classmate?

Initially students' entries in online discussions will vary considerably in length, quality, and depth of disclosure. Students are aware that everyone in the class is reading their entries, and most will not choose to become too personal or disclosing in this initial posting. However, if the bio assignment is well constructed, even a cursory response begins to tell the instructor how the student fares against the risk profile discussed earlier. How is the student's writing? Has he been out of school for several years? Is she working full-time? Is the student independent? With children? Attending full or part time? Even single-parent status is likely to come out in this initial biography, and a few unobtrusive questions can fill in gaps in the profile. Here are two examples of typical student profiles, based on the assignment provided previously:

Terence

This is Terence. I go by Terence. I'm 19 and was born and raised in Chicago. How would I describe myself? I live for baseball. I'm a freshman here playing baseball, and that's how I think about myself and mainly all I do when I'm not in class. So I'm a fulltime student and have a work-study job over at the gym and keeping up the field. I also like my music! Raking the field with my MP3 player. That's me.

I have three brothers back in Chicago, and my mom, and I'm the oldest. I'm taking this class 'cause Coach put it on my schedule and I can fit it around my games and practices. I don't know about this taking a class online, but I made it through the little test class I had to do. What do I want to do when I get out of here? You no [sic] it. Play baseball. So—now you no [sic] Terence.

Cyndi

Hi! My name is Cyndi and I was born here in Springfield and have lived here all my life. This is my second semester here and my first online class and I have to admit I'm pretty nervous about it. I'm not what you would call a real computer whiz and I hope I can figure out everything I need to do for this class! I would describe myself as a person who really loves animals, and has a good way with them.

I work in the afternoons at Wal-Mart as a checker, and have been an associate for four years. It's not a bad job, but I want to get into management, and need at least an associate degree to get the position I want. I'm taking two classes this semester—this one and Freshman Comp II—and with my work, it's going to be a real challenge.

I love to ride horses in my spare time—what there is of it!—and do things with my daughter Jeryn, who is five and just started half-day kindergarten. We have a horse that we keep at my parent's place north of town, and try to ride on weekend.

I'm taking this class mainly because it's required (I've got to be honest about it!), and I figured the online would let me work on it at about any time, and not have to have so much babysitting between when Jeryn gets home and when I go to work at 3:00. How would I like to spend my time? Being a good mom and having a place in the country where my daughter can grow up enjoying being outdoors. I guess that's about it!

———————————

From these relatively brief responses, the teacher learns that without some coaching, Terence is going to be brief, and Cyndi chatty. Terence may not be highly motivated as a student, but he is motivated by baseball. Cyndi has specific goals and probably manages her time well. Cyndi is high on the risk factor chart—a part-time student, probably working full time, out of school for several years, with a dependent child. She also may be a single mother. But Terence may have risk factors that are more critical, even though he is enrolled full time and is of traditional age. Baseball consumes much of his week. His work–study eligibility and the indication that he is from a single-parent family, with three brothers still at home, indicate that he may have significant financial need. A quick look at the rest of his schedule will let the instructor know

what kind of developmental course load he is carrying, if any.

Cyndi's response to a brief follow-up e-mail might provide a clearer sense of her schedule and motivation: "Hi Cyndi. Welcome to the class! Wow! I'm impressed with all you are trying to do! When do you find time to study with all the other demands in your life?" And Terence might immediately feel more a part of the class with a brief, "Terence, glad to have you in class. What position do you play, and what kind of music do you like? Let me know when you have home games, and I'll see if I can get over to one."

Collison, Elbaum, Haavind, and Tinker (2000) indicated that this initial socialization process in an online setting is particularly important in that it begins to build a sense of community among students in the absence of the physical community of a traditional classroom. If nurtured properly, this community can be as supportive and close as any the student experiences.

Community College Students as Online Learners

Credible research on how community college students respond to online learning is scant and often inconclusive. A small institutional study completed by Patrick Henry Community College indicated that participation in some distance learning courses actually increased persistence to graduation. But when students took more than five courses through distance learning, retention began to drop (K. Shropshire, personal communication, October 17, 2005). These data lead to speculation about whether comparable, effective, appropriate, and adequate support systems are in place for students with heavy distance learning loads. They also suggest follow-up questions about whether students carrying a high number of distance learning hours are more likely to have more risk factors than are other students.

Carnwell (cited in Wheeler, 2002) identified categories of support required of distance learning students. She suggested that of the three identified— practical (administrative), emotional, and academic—some students require all three, whereas others may need only one or two. Research by Moore (1989), Saba (1988), Wheeler (2002), and others indicate that students' perceptions of distance are more a reflection of psychological than of geographic separation. When appropriate dialogue and course structure bring learner and instructor together, much of the sense of distance can be removed.

Moore identified three critical interactions in distance learning environments—learner–content, learner–instructor, and learner–learner—and suggested that the learner–instructor interaction is the most critical in closing perceived distance. Further evidence shows that this interaction becomes most effective when it is frequent and when student recipients are addressed by name (Moore, 1989). This is a relatively simple concept to understand when you consider that computer-savvy students in the face-to-face setting of a traditional classroom are often able to maintain considerable psychological distance between themselves and an instructor. They can remain remote, disconnected, and isolated while sitting in the middle of a room full of peers. These same students have the ability, however, to establish very close personal relationships with online friends, many of whom they have never met. The online environment can, in fact, make establishing "psychological closeness" easier for teachers in certain situations than can the on-ground classroom. Students who lack some of the affective skills that Kemp (2002) identified will not feel the need to hide in an online classroom and can more easily be engaged in an exchange with the instructor and with other students.

In chapters 7 and 8, where we discuss managing online classes effectively, we suggest that instructors refrain from becoming overly involved in classroom discussion so as not to stifle or inhibit candid dialogue. This may appear contradictory to the advice just given, but these chapters explain that the two suggestions are not mutually exclusive. There are a number of ways to remain close to students without being a controlling presence in class discussion. Several of these student contact strategies will be reviewed in later chapters and can be very helpful in closing psychological distance.

Teaching Tip

Make a personal contact with each student through a letter, e-mail, or phone call to communicate that you are a real person; invite each student to communicate with you. Just because you do not see students in class each week does not mean you do not expect to hear from them. Ask students for their expectations of the online course. Point out misunderstandings in the beginning.

—*Jo Ann Armstrong*
online psychology and sociology instructor
Patrick Henry Community College, Virginia

Early Personal Contact

One technique that bears mention here is the strategy of sending an introductory letter to each student before the semester begins. This letter should tell a little about yourself and explain how to access the class and begin work. This letter will be discussed in detail in chapter 6, with an accompanying example. Regular, personalized announcements when students log into the class site also can establish a sense of connection without being overly time-consuming. Suggestions for using the announcement section of the online platform are part of the discussion in chapter 7.

A well-constructed introductory letter and regular announcement postings will keep students' e-mails to a minimum. Nevertheless, nothing will affect the student's sense of distance more quickly than will the timeliness of your response to e-mail. In the course syllabus, students should be made aware of how quickly they can expect an e-mail response and should be informed if circumstances alter that schedule. You can, as an effective communicator, respond quickly and personally to students' e-mails without encouraging a regular contact relationship simply by speaking to students by name but directing them to resources other than e-mail exchanges to resolve future questions.

A student may, for example, send a note asking how he or she is to organize a case study analysis you have assigned. Your response might be as follows:

Sandy, I'm glad to see you're interested in getting this format just right and are concerned about the organization of your analysis. I anticipated that students might need additional help in this area. In the syllabus, at the end of the assignment description for the case study, you will find information about how to organize this assignment. Some additional material in the Unit 1 folder provides examples as well. I will generally try to have examples of assignments in the unit folders. So, when you have a format or style question, take a look there and see if you find what you need. If not, please get back with me. Again, Sandy, I appreciate the effort to get the analysis in the right format!

The Millennials

Community college enrollments are now burgeoning with a group that some academic analysts believe will change the face of higher education—and add even greater pressure for online and other creative delivery approaches. Labeled the "millennials" or the "Net generation," these students were born during the last two decades of the 20th century. Richard T. Sweeney, university librarian at the New Jersey Institute of Technology, has been lecturing nationally about the emergence of millennials as a student type and about the need to modify both our approaches to instruction and our willingness to accept how learning occurs. Carlson (2005) alerted us to their presence by beginning an article about the generation in the *Chronicle of Higher Education* with this message from Sweeney:

Change your teaching style. Make blogs, iPods, and video games part of your pedagogy. And learn to accept divided attention spans. A new generation of students has arrived—and sorry, but they might not want to hear you lecture for an hour. (p. A34)

Millennials are characterized in the article as multitasking to the point that they appear inattentive, occasionally rude, and as having brief attention spans. Students in this group choose to describe themselves differently. They acknowledge that they might not prefer to learn in the traditional ways— sitting in lecture halls and listening to lengthy discourses by professors on the stage. However, they are voracious learners, using resources they feel too many instructors fail to make available. They are inclined to want to shape their own majors based on where they see the job market going, do not see any particular value in traditional attendance expectations as long as they are learning the material, and would prefer to learn from each other and from a variety of media sources than from a professor. Carlson, quoting Sweeney, said of millennials,

They have no brand loyalty . . . They "accept as their right" the ability to make choices and customize the things they choose. They are more educated than their parents and expect to make more money. "Many more have changed majors and expect to change jobs and careers". . . But they often wait until they are already well into a major or a career track before they decide to make a change . . . Playing with gizmos and digital technology is second nature to them. "They like portability, and they are frustrated by technology that tethers them to a specific location,". . . Studies show that Millennials don't read as much as previous generations did. They prefer video, audio, and interactive media. They multitask. "They are much more likely to mix work and play than we are . . . playing a game or chatting while they are doing an assignment. In grade school, they were pushed to collaboration," which explains the popularity of group study in college today . . . "The Collaboration . . . is both person and virtual . . . they want to learn, but they want to learn only what they have to learn, and they want to learn it in a style that is best for them"... Often they prefer to learn by doing. (Carlson, 2005, p. A34)

Although the interests of the Net generation add to the critical importance of making online and other learning modalities available, they at once complicate the challenges facing community college faculty teaching in the Web-based environment. Millennials will constitute only a portion of your enrollment in a given class. The rest will be generation Xers, baby boomers, and every group in between, and all will have specific interests and learning preferences. But millennials will have high expectations concerning technology, will welcome a less structured learning environment, and will embrace active, collaborative learning.

It is not, of course, your responsibility as an instructor to mitigate for every difficulty students in your classes experience or every learning preference they may express. There is a significant school of thought, in fact, that argues that we have some responsibility to "mold how they learn" (Baron, cited in Carlson, 2005). We are among those who believe that part of our responsibilities as teachers is to prepare students for a world that does not always conform to their leaning styles, their preferred time schedules, and their favorite ways of accessing and processing information. There are, nonetheless, opportunities unique to the online environment to capitalize on learning interests that make the experience more meaningful and productive for those you teach. In the next four chapters, you will learn about a number of tools that can add to your success as a master facilitator of online learning, and you will find examples of strategies that aid in accommodating the needs of this highly diverse community college student population.

The most important tool for every student's success, however, is not in the computer, but in the teacher. Cynthia Arem, who teaches psychology online for Pima Community College in Arizona, summed this up nicely:

Be there for your students. Many students believe that their teacher is on the "other-side" of their computer screen. So it is important to check your e-mail every day, and even several times a day (during the work week), if you can . . . Answer your students' e-mail promptly. If you don't know the answer, let them know you will get back to them with the answer as soon as you can . . . Always be **extra** friendly in your emails. Without face-to-face contact, emails can seem cold to students. Thank students for emailing you or for asking questions (even if the answers are in your syllabus). A friendly attitude in your emails will get much better responses from your students. Always try to use welcoming salutations and pleasant closings. In addition, it helps to sometimes send friendly messages to the class. For example, a "Happy Thanksgiving" or "Happy Valentine's Day" message can make the course seem much warmer to students. (C. Arem, personal communication, December 15, 2005)

It is in the personal approach to each student that psychological distance begins to disappear and a learning community develops. We must caution, though, that as in the traditional classroom, you must find a way to maintain that balance between personal attention and overfamiliarity. Overfamiliarity not only can cross the bounds of professional distance but also can encourage some students to create dependencies that ultimately prove unhealthy for all. However, the online environment can become a warm and inviting one, and once engaged in an exciting community of learners, students can overcome what appear monumental obstacles and do remarkable things.

Online Orientation

In this chapter, we outline the need for and advantages of a good online orientation and the merit of requiring an orientation before course work begins. A Web-based orientation can aid students in determining whether their equipment meets the requirements of the college's courses, how ably they can navigate in the online environment, and how the platform used by the college works. Orientations address many of the questions that students often have initially, thereby saving the instructor time answering inquiries after the course begins.

In the previous chapter, several suggestions were made about using biographies to get to know students better, anticipate their learning challenges, and create varied approaches to instruction. These activities add time to course preparation and delivery, but from the beginning, we have stressed that online teaching is time intensive. That makes it even more critical that your time be committed to constructive teaching and learning activities and not to procedural demands created by the learning format.

Among the most useful aids to saving valuable instruction time is a well-developed and well-delivered online student orientation. We cannot emphasize strongly enough that an orientation should be mandatory for all students taking their first online course. If an institution does not provide a required online orientation, it is doing both its faculty and students a great disservice. Most automated registration systems allow students to be flagged and prevented from registering if they have not completed a prerequisite. It is a

relatively simple process for an online orientation to be constructed as a prerequisite so that when students successfully complete it, an automatic code appears in the registration system that allows the student to enroll in Web-based courses, but not before.

Orientation Elements

The online orientation should have three major objectives: to assess students' equipment and software, to evaluate students' abilities as they relate to online learning, and to review the essential tools used by the college's course management system or delivery platform. The first objective allows students to see how well adapted their equipment is to the demands of an online course. It should include a basic checklist of necessary hardware and software, Internet connectivity requirements, e-mail access, and the like. Some faculty members will develop specific additional requirements if special software is needed, but every online course offered by the college

Online Orientation Examples

College of DuPage
www.cod.edu/online

Columbia Basin College
www.columbiabasin.edu

Crowder College
www.crowder.edu/on_line_classes.html

Illinois Online Network
www.ion.uillinois.edu/resources/tutorials

Sauk Valley Community College
http://intserver.svcc.edu/orientation

Sinclair Community College
www.sinclair.edu/stservices/enrl/orientation

Southwest Technical College
www.swtc.edu/online_learning/
orientation/index.htm

will have basic requirements. These requirements should be made clear in the orientation.

The orientation also should notify students if some basic hardware or connectivity, although acceptable as a bare minimum, would make it difficult to complete assignments in a timely fashion. For example, students should be informed that dialup modems or Internet connections with limited speed will create challenges in sending and receiving large files, including streaming audio and video. In addition, file attachments to some commercial e-mail systems such as Hotmail are often filtered carefully by Internet security screeners to protect against the transmission of viruses. Students using these e-mail services might run into transmission problems. Students deserve to be made aware of any characteristic of the college information technology network that may create special challenges based on equipment and connectivity.

Orientation Examples

The second critical element of an orientation is to familiarize students with skills needed to successfully navigate the course and complete assignments. The following are some examples of how several colleges

present online orientations. Two of the examples used in this chapter are from Illinois—a credit perhaps to the exceptional online networking resources made available by the University of Illinois through the Illinois Online Network. At the network's Web site, online faculty and students can find information about virtually every aspect of Web-based instruction, from course development, to student assessment, to pedagogy and learning. The site also includes an excellent section on what makes a successful online student, presenting a list of questions and characteristics that appear in many of the Illinois orientation programs.

Crowder College

The online orientation at Crowder College in Missouri begins with a list of hardware and software requirements. It then presents a list of abilities or skills that will be helpful for online success:

- Does the user know how to access the Internet?
- Is he or she proficient in using a Web browser?
- Can he or she send and receive e-mail, including attachments?
- Is the student proficient in using a word-processing program?

Teaching Tip

I begin each online class with a few exercises for students to complete to be sure an online class is right for them. I have them practice using a bulletin board, sending the entire class an e-mail via our online mailing list, and finally, completing an online questionnaire for potential online students. One of the best models is provided by the Illinois Online Network: www.ion.uillinois.edu/resources/tutorials/pedagogy/selfEval.asp.

—*Chris Rubio*
online English instructor
American River College, California

The college also provides a simple self-scored assessment that suggests, based on score, whether the student (a) probably is well suited to Web-based instruction, (b) probably is able to manage an online course effectively but will need extra help and can expect additional work, or (c) probably should not consider online instruction without significant additional skill development. This orientation is now part of the college's general freshman seminar class, taking the majority of new full-time students through the orientation early, whether or not they are planning on an online course.

This movement beyond equipment needs, to important personal skills, highlights the need for the orientation to acquaint students with the demands and expectations of online course work. Each orientation should provide a self-assessment that helps students determine whether they are suited to this learning approach. You can view a number of orientation programs on the Web that provide good examples of this second requirement.

College of DuPage

The orientation provided by Illinois' College of DuPage presents a simple eight-step process. Steps 1 and 2 focus on determining whether equipment is suitable and whether taking an online course is a wise choice. The second step then directs students to an attachment that poses questions for the prospective online learner to consider:

- Do you have self-discipline and motivation?
- Are you able to commit time each day or week to your online course(s)?
- Do you have good communication skills and enjoy expressing your ideas in writing?
- Do you feel comfortable discussing problems with your instructors?
- Will you miss the experience of sitting in a classroom?
- Are you comfortable with computers?

The DuPage orientation also provides a brief self-assessment of both the personal characteristics of a

---

> ## Teaching Tip
>
> I tell students considering an online class that they need to have good reading skills and good self-discipline to learn in this environment. On the opening page of the course description, I tell them that an online class is more work, in many ways, than an on-ground class, and then I give them an overview of what they can expect.
>
> —*Jane Schreck*
> *online English instructor*
> *Bismarck State College, North Dakota*

---

successful online learner and the student's technical readiness for Web-based instruction.

Southwest Technical College

Students seeking information about online courses at Southwest Technical College in Wisconsin are greeted with a boldfaced message that declares, "You will not be granted access to participate in online courses until you have successfully completed the Online Orientation." This college offers more than 100 courses online, and, in its orientation, it expands on the personal skills inventory to provide students with additional information about time management, study skills, and learning styles. After each learning module, students are directed to brief assignments that assess their knowledge of the topic and are asked for their own evaluation of their preparation. These assessments are attached to an e-mail and sent to an orientation facilitator who reviews results and can advise students about specific needs or weaknesses.

Sauk Valley Community College

An excellent illustration of three elements of an effective orientation is the program provided by Sauk Valley Community College in Dixon, Illinois. Sauk Valley uses WebCT (described in detail in chapter 10) as its delivery platform, and the college Web site allows students to download an online learning guide in either Windows

> **Teaching Tip**
>
> I require students to take a tutorial class before starting the online class.
>
> *—Edith Shaked*
> *online history instructor*
> *Pima Community College, Arizona*

or Macintosh format. Much of the focus of this guide is on the third essential element of a good online orientation: acquainting the student with the college's online platform and how to navigate the course software.

But the orientation begins, in this case, not by asking questions about the student's hardware and software, but by taking the prospective online learner through a series of exercises and equipment tests that check the hardware directly. Students are asked, "when you click here, do you see the described image? Does it move? Can you view the brief video? If not, click here to see if you can download the needed software that will allow your system to work." If technical assistance is needed, an e-mail address and phone number are provided to put the student in touch with someone who can help. If the student's computer can perform the needed functions, the orientation advances to a set of exercises using WebCT, and the student gains direct experience with the course management system before enrolling in any course.

> **Teaching Tip**
>
> Students need to evaluate themselves in several areas concerning their readiness for online learning. They should be a good time manager, be self-motivated, and possess good technology skills. They also need to blend online learning into their already busy lives and learn to enjoy the process.
>
> *—Dee Ludwig*
> *online human development instructor*
> *Eastern Wyoming College, Wyoming*

Developing an Orientation

With our counsel that an online orientation is a must, what do you do if your college does not offer one? Our recommendation is that you find a way to provide it. Begin by approaching your IT staff or department about creating an orientation using an existing orientation as a model. Community colleges are inclined to share, and nothing will be lost by approaching colleges that have good programs and asking that they make them available to you.

Should your IT person or department decline to create a program, you can create your own or develop one cooperatively with your online colleagues, then require students entering your courses for the first time to go through it before beginning class. There are several models you might look at that provide a simple template, using basic word processing or presentation software skills. For example, on its main Web page menu, Columbia Basin College has a selection for eLearning that includes submenus for its eLearning orientation schedule, with information about successful online learner profiles and strategies for success. Even if the eLearning orientation were not available, its list of success elements, taken from the work of Osborne (2001) and Muse (2004) could be a useful prerequisite review for online students. They note that the successful distance learner at Columbia Basin

- Has more previous education than an at-risk (online) student
- Has a higher grade point average than an at-risk student
- Has a good study environment (time and place to do school work)
- Is older
- Is taking fewer credits and working more hours than an at-risk student
- Is returning to college after more than 2 years away
- Is highly motivated
- Has already completed a distance class
- Gets support from family and friends
- Is confident using computers

Teaching Tip

Do not assume that all of your students know how to use the various online communication methods. Be willing to provide them with detailed instructions as needed, and walk your students through the processes you intend to use for your class. It may take a couple of tries with each method for some of your students. During the semester, my online students submit a series of exercises that use increasingly complicated submission formats: e-mail response, e-mail response with a suitable word-processed attachment, e-mail with digital photo attachment, cutting and pasting between the assignment handout and material submission, discussion board, and digital drop box (submission and recovery of files).

—*Herb Schade*
online physical science instructor
Crowder College, Missouri

This information is followed by a set of success strategies that include details about the technology, scheduling, and getting connected.

Sinclair Community College in Ohio presents its orientation for students using an online format. It is a simple PowerPoint presentation that walks students step by step through the institution and its services, finishing with a brief quiz. You can view this presentation on Sinclair's Web site and can create a similar orientation for new online students on a Web site without the interactivity of the more elaborate models described previously. The orientation should, however, include the three requisites:

- An opportunity to assess student equipment (hardware and software) and determine its suitability to basic online course requirements.
- An opportunity to gain an understanding of the demands and expectations of online course work.
- An opportunity to become acquainted with the essentials of the college's online platform (course

management program such as Blackboard or WebCT) and information about what students will find when they enter the course.

Removing the Fear

The most effective orientation will be created around the "rule of no surprises." When students first enter the course, everything should look familiar, and no task should require major additional instruction to complete. To illustrate with a more personal example, an associate who was a former Air Force pilot related the experience of enduring Air Force Survival School. The training culminated in a simulated evasion, capture, and imprisonment that included considerable physical discomfort, sleeplessness, and aggressive interrogation. At the conclusion of the exercise, one participant asked those directing the camp if it was necessary that it be that realistic! The officer in charge answered that years of experience had shown that fear and failure are directly related in degree and intensity to being faced with the unknown. Remove the unknown, and much of the fear and likelihood of failure disappear.

We do not, of course, want to compare taking an online course with serving in combat or with enemy capture. However, a little "survival school" beforehand

Teaching Tip

Practice makes perfect. Establish orientation sessions for guided exploration of the course management tools for new users. Consider setting up a sample course for students to log into before the semester begins. Having their initial e-mail directed to either the instructor or a department representative who responds in kind can begin the cycle of communication and feedback that students come to rely on in the online environment.

—*Susan Holmes*
online communications instructor
NorthWest Arkansas Community College

will have many of the same values. Students entering your course who immediately feel at home with the technology and the demands of the assignments can immediately dedicate their energies to engaging in other elements of the learning environment and will save you untold hours of frustration.

CHAPTER 5

Who Should Teach Online— and Who Shouldn't

In this chapter, we explain why online instruction ideally meets the teaching needs of many departments and instructors, allowing faculty to be on campus, at home, or in Timbuktu. Web-based instruction allows colleges to extend their teaching base across the country and around the world, adding diversity and experience where it may not exist in the community. We also explain that online instruction may improve some teachers' effectiveness, whereas others will find that they are not suited to Web-based delivery.

It is unrealistic to suggest that everyone can be an effective online teacher and facilitator. Not everyone can be an effective teacher, and the online environment adds a number of complicating circumstances that make it even more critical to self-evaluate suitability for this approach. It is equally true that some faculty may be better suited to online teaching and learning than to the traditional classroom, and a teacher who struggles in front of a live class may come alive in a Web-based course.

Characteristics of Capable Teachers

Collison et al. (2000), in *Facilitating Online Learning: Effective Strategies for Moderators*, reviewed a series of characteristics for successful online instruction gleaned from years of work with the International Network Teacher Enhancement Coalition (INTEC). They noted that

while we're a long way from developing a profile of characteristics or attributes pos-

sessed by skilled online moderators, humility, the capacity to listen (read!) carefully, and the ability to respond without interjecting personal or professional opinions or values appear to be characteristics shared by most successful practitioners. (Collison et al., 2000, p. xvi)

They emphasized the importance of the instructor in this setting serving as the "guide on the side" rather than as the more traditional "sage on the stage." Teachers should use their skills to focus or redirect discussion as needed and to maintain what Collison et al. referred to as "pragmatic dialogue" rather than engaging in contrasting "social" or "argumentative" discussion.

There are occasions and proper places for social dialogue in an online course; we will discuss those more fully in chapter 8. For our purposes, we define social dialogue simply as discussion that is unrelated to the specific content of the course. Argumentative

Teaching Tip

Be willing to make mistakes, admit them, learn from them, and then move on from them. This also sends a tremendous message to students that you are human. Be willing to commit your time, energy, and expertise to the course. Be ready, willing, and able to make several tweaks and adjustments before, during, and after each course offered online. I do this with almost every class. Be willing to give up more control of the class to the students—of course, with your direction and guidance.

—Joe Ellefson
online criminal justice instructor
Bismarck State College, North Dakota

dialogue is manifested in a number of ways—as advocacy, as diversion, or as an attempt to slow discussion. A skilled online instructor must not only avoid these temptations personally but also be able to recognize them in the contributions of others and assist students toward more pragmatic discussion.

Collison and his colleagues acknowledged that

> though social and argumentative forms of dialogue are present in most discourse, the intention of pragmatic dialogue—time-limited, product-driven dialogue that is critically sensitive to collaboration and the use of each participant's personal resources—provides a framework for the goal-directed conversations needed in online courses . . . (2000, p. 30)

Pragmatic discourse serves to build a learning community by creating a sense of safety and discovery among participants while establishing a climate of respect and reasoned discussion. Collison et al. noted that the goal as facilitator is to support the intellectual content of the course by maintaining a forward direction for the dialogue and stated that

you must focus emerging ideas and juxtapose emerging tensions. Participants then sense forward direction in the form of greater clarity, richer content or context, a deeper personal vision or an engagement with the goals of the course through the process of inquiry. (2000, p. 31)

The instructor's role also becomes one of introducing related lines of thought, broadening the field of discussion, and relating participants' contributions to the central theme. This adds to the creation of a general sense of ownership in the discussion. This approach to creating "learning community" requires special skills on the part of the instructor—skills that even an experienced classroom teacher may or may not possess, including the following:

- To write clearly and be able to communicate the nuances of intent and meaning critical to managing the delicate tasks of focusing, juxtaposing, and introducing tangential thought
- To question without appearing to be challenging or adversarial
- To project your personality through written connections and to enhance the students' feeling of having "real people" in the learning community

These are talents that can be honed over time but that require a basic ability to communicate sensitively in writing. There is also a set of more mundane skills needed in the online environment—skills that are perhaps more a reflection of personal discipline than of instructional style or inclination. To be effective online, the teacher must

- Be comfortable with computers and basic software
- Be a regular and dependable online correspondent
- Be willing and able to commit time almost daily to the online course

Figure 5.1. Self-assessment of online readiness.

		Yes	No
1.	I feel comfortable with basic computer use for e-mail and word processing.	❏	❏
2.	I can comfortably attach documents to online correspondence and can change word formatting if needed.	❏	❏
3.	I am able to access information on the Web and can insert Web links into documents.	❏	❏
4.	I am willing to experiment with new computer technologies and tools.	❏	❏
5.	I check e-mail regularly and respond quickly.	❏	❏
6.	I am able to communicate my ideas, feelings, and interests effectively in writing.	❏	❏
7.	I am able to guide and focus discussion without controlling and imposing a certain perspective.	❏	❏
8.	I recognize related threads in discussion and am able to integrate ideas.	❏	❏
9.	I feel comfortable in the role of guide and facilitator rather than "teacher" and expert.	❏	❏
10.	I can spend several hours working online on a regular basis.	❏	❏

If teaching online, you will be expecting students to participate in the course four or five times a week. Realizing that they will not all be involved on the same days or at the same times, your personal expectation needs to include almost daily involvement if you are to keep the dialogue moving forward appropriately.

Jim Burns, who teaches online English at Mountain Empire Community College in Big Stone Gap, Virginia, advises that a good online instructor should be highly accessible to the students. This does not mean 24/7 duty, but it does mean answering students' e-mail questions promptly and letting students know when instructors are available (J. Burns, personal communication, December 8, 2005). Online office hours seldom work in the asynchronous online class. Instead, students should be given realistic and honest indications of how quickly and at what times of the day and week instructors will respond.

Online Readiness Checklist

Figure 5.1 shows a 10-item checklist that will allow you to assess your readiness to be effective as an online instructor. It is not a scored evaluation that provides a cut-off, indicating that you should or should not teach online. It is designed instead to help you assess areas in which you will need to improve or receive additional training to teach successfully in this environment.

Some of the skills noted in this assessment are acquired easily. For example, if you are not able to attach documents to e-mail messages, insert Web links into text, or change text formatting, someone with these abilities can teach you in a matter of minutes. Other abilities, such as the skill to guide and focus ideas without controlling and imposing a perspective, may be more difficult to develop. Here, you might approach a colleague who is particularly adept at integrating discussion

Teaching Tip

What makes an effective online teacher?

- Clear instructions

- Prompt response to students' questions

- Empathy and kindness with students' difficulties

- Diversity in assignments

- A clear and detailed syllabus

- Weekly e-mails to all students, introduction to the module, and reminder e-mails

- Always reading students' critique at the end of the semester and being ready to make changes, accordingly.

—Edith Shaked
online history instructor
Pima Community College, AZ

and ask for assistance or request that your professional development staff create a workshop focusing on these abilities. Later in this chapter, we recommend faculty orientation and on-going professional development for online instructors and suggest that both include opportunities to develop or hone these skills.

There may be some instructors who complete this assessment who do not see it as their role as a teacher to integrate, guide, and introduce related themes. They believe they are in front of the class to instruct and inform—the traditional "pour information into the funnel and hope some sticks" approach. Faculty with this perspective will face the same limitations online that they do in the classroom.

These faculty lose much of the advantage online learning provides—greater deliberation during threaded discussion as students express and develop ideas and greater exploration of the endless resources instantly accessible to learners in the online environment. Students also will find these faculty especially frustrating in that without the opportunity to engage

in regular and meaningful discussion, the sense of distance created by distance learning becomes all the greater.

Who Should Not Teach Online?

Are there faculty who absolutely should not teach online? Teachers who never return assignments, fail to provide feedback on projects, and refuse to get grades in on time—who suffer from general inattention to the learning needs of students—will fail as online teachers. Web-based learning compounds the problems of faculty irresponsibility and leaves students feeling completely abandoned and afloat in educational cyberspace, with nowhere to turn.

Academic administrators occasionally see online teaching as instructional limbo—a place to send faculty who are receiving poor classroom evaluations and peer reviews. In other cases, weak teachers seek refuge in what they hope will be the anonymity of the online classroom. Both of these shelters, when used to compensate for personal irresponsibility and conscious lack of attention to students and their learning, are acts of academic malpractice and should never be tolerated.

Who Can Be More Effective Online?

There are, nonetheless, those situations in which certain faculty members prove to be more effective online than they are in the traditional classroom. Some are more skilled at organizing their thoughts in written form. Others find the pace of the face-to-face classroom a difficult forum in which to formulate integrated responses or to redirect and focus discussion. But given the extra time allowed by the asynchronous nature of Web-based teaching, these faculty members are able to be much more insightful.

There is also that teacher who has an imaginative flair with technology who will "catch fire" when presented with the endless possibilities afforded by online learning. Granted, the addition of technology such as Smart Boards and computer projection systems allow for much of the same innovation in the classroom. However, often this techno-whiz is much more comfortable sitting in front of a computer than standing before a Smart Board. He or she may also be perfectly suited to the interests of the millennials or Net generation who were discussed in chapter 3 and are looking for faculty who enjoy communicating as they do.

Students born between 1980 and 1994 have been described as tech savvy, smart but impatient, and plugged in electronically. According to an article in the *The Chronicle of Higher Education* titled "The Net Generation Goes to College," this group is "expecting to be able to choose what kind of education they buy, and what, where, and how they learn" (Carlson, 2005, p. A34). We are asked to

> imagine classrooms that incorporate more video and video games; classes that meet electronically to fit students' schedules, students who choose to learn from each other rather than a professor, and courseware. Search engines, and library databases that are animated, image-based, and interactive. (Carlson, 2005, p. A34)

Carlson asserted that there is need for a breed of professors who understand the millennials and their desire to "learn from a wide variety of media, often simultaneously" (Carlson, 2005, p. A34). The teacher who can adapt to this format, address the needs of this emerging student group, and still accommodate the learning styles and interests of the

---

Teaching Tip

Avoid making a chilly impression. Research has shown that what we type online is not quite what we would say in person. Use simple phrases to express more agreement than disagreement, and make an effort to use civilities that are common in most interactions.

—*Jo Ann Armstrong*
online psychology and sociology instructor
Patrick Henry Community College, Virginia

---

nonmillennials in the class, is a rare find indeed. Academic leaders in this case will need to be cautious, however, that their techno-whiz instructors do not outpace the technological abilities and equipment of the students.

Institutions also may find that some faculty with disabilities have gifts that provide them with special talents in the online environment. Hearing- or speech-impaired teachers, for example, often become especially adept at nonverbal forms of expression and have special talents for building learning communities in the written world.

Finding Online Faculty

The possibilities of online instruction should encourage academic administrators to take a fresh look at who is now available to teach but was not before. The miracle of the Internet and asynchronous learning is that time and distance no longer matter. Faculty who wish to spend a few years away from the classroom to be with a growing family may still be interested in teaching a course from home. That star American history professor who retired and moved to her cottage on the lake is no longer out of reach. Nor is the geologist from Amoco or the senior State Department officer who retired to Florida. The agricultural economist who would love to teach a course but is traveling abroad too often to meet with an evening class on a regular basis is now a potential adjunct professor, as is the former student who went on to law school and now works for the U.S. Patent Attorney's office in Washington, DC. The more remote the teaching staff is, the greater the challenges of teacher training and evaluation, but these challenges are not insurmountable.

Instructor Orientation

Let us again reinforce a message that has been a theme throughout. Teaching online is not simply a matter of transferring old techniques and old course content into a Web-based course management system. It is thinking about how learning can be accommodated in creative, stimulating new ways using the special advantages the online forum provides. Those who teach most successfully online are those who approach the challenge and

Teaching Tip

Being able to communicate beyond any boundaries is a key talent associated with great online instructors. Connecting to students who have chosen to study at a distance requires placing priorities on communication and feedback.

—*Susan Holmes*
online communications instructor
NorthWest Arkansas Community College

opportunity with that goal in mind and with an enthusiasm for learning from the process.

The institutions that will have the best corps of online teachers will be those who provide thorough and applicable online training for all who teach in this environment. This orientation should include all of the elements that are part of the student orientation—how to use essential computer tools and the features provided by the institution's course management system. It also should school the faculty in the techniques and teaching approaches that are particularly important to online instruction. These should include the following abilities to

- Manage technological challenges
- Present detailed written instructions that are readable, interesting, and clear
- Access, evaluate, and make available to students the wealth of information
- Available on the Web
- Facilitate effective online discussion
- Form and use online student groups
- Create collaborative activities that involve students in teaching each other

Faculty Support Groups

If the college does not provide formal orientation or ongoing professional development for faculty, we recommend that you take the initiative to create your own faculty support group. This collaboration may be the most effective way to create a simple student orientation that you can all use, and it will at least serve to bring together your online teaching colleagues on a regular basis to exchange ideas, share concerns, and help each other with new technologies and teaching techniques. You should include colleagues who are not part of the on-campus teaching staff by using the tools you use in your courses: virtual classroom and synchronous messaging functions. Our experience has been that these sessions are most successful if they are structured, with assignments to specific faculty to make presentations about a tool, discuss a teaching strategy, or review useful online resources.

One community college had each of its first cadre of online faculty take a Web course together on how to teach online. They then used this core team as trainers for teachers who later joined the online ranks. Jim Burns of Mountain Empire Community College recommended, "Take an online course yourself. The best thing instructors can do to help prepare their students for the online learning experience is to learn for themselves what it is like to be an online student" (personal communication, December 8, 2005).

Most important, realize that as you move into the online environment—and as you continue to work there—you must become a learner yourself. Take advantage of this new opportunity as you would expect the best of your students to approach your classes: with openness, curiosity, a willingness to study hard and take risks, and a constant interest in discovering new things.

CHAPTER 6

Laying the Groundwork

In this chapter, we describe a precourse letter that directs new students into your course platform and puts them in touch with resources that will help them get started. We explain how to prepare an effective syllabus and create learning seminars that break down the course into manageable units.

The old axiom that "a stitch in time saves nine" has never been more true than in its application to preparing students to enter and navigate an online course. By telling students well before the course begins what to expect and when to expect it, then by repeating these instructions regularly in obvious places, you can save hours of time once the course is under way. Successful online instructor Jane Schreck of Bismarck State College advises, "repeat, repeat, repeat!" (J. Schreck, personal communication, December 7, 2005). A well-developed orientation begins this process, but after entering the online classroom, each student is faced with your particular approach to the class and with your group of assignments and activities.

Course Size

Before getting into the specifics of the course, we need to make an observation about class size. Online courses in colleges and universities range in size from a dozen to several hundred students. The larger classes usually exist at universities, where they replace general education sections of equivalent size when taught in the traditional lecture hall. This kind of course delivery is not consistent with the community college philosophy of care and concern. A huge online course is generally nothing more than a large lecture course transplanted to the Web, with weekly readings and lectures and assignments graded by graduate assistants. Our belief is that if properly delivered, online courses are as time intensive as the most demanding sections offered on campus and should be treated in the same way when developing faculty load. Limitations typically placed on English composition class sizes may serve as a reasonable standard for online courses as well. There should be an expectation that faculty members teaching online will spend equivalent time reading students' entries, facilitating discussion, and managing the system.

Administrators might respond by suggesting that online courses lose some of their institutional value if limited to sizes that are smaller than sections of the same course offered on-ground. If institutional value is measured in terms of tuition and generated student enrollment, this might be true. However, if value is measured in terms of access, accommodation, and application of sound

Teaching Tip

Repeat it! Give detailed information in your syllabus on everything from textbooks to tests, from course expectations to grading scale. Then do the same thing for each unit or chapter of study. Use the same format for each one. (If you have a heading of Assignments, Notes, PowerPoint, Summary, and Quiz in Unit #1, follow the same format for each unit.)

I cannot stress enough that you need to be specific in your syllabus, content, general instructions, and individual instructions. If you think students can't possibly mistake what you are saying, I am here to testify that yes, they can. Most of the time however, they are doing it just the way you said they should. We always know what we intended to say and write. If you are not sure it is clear, give it to somebody unfamiliar with the course and content and see whether they understand it. If not, start tweaking.

Even if you make yourself sound like a real hard case, be strict in your syllabus. You can always soften a little as the case may need, but you can never make your requirements or standards harder after the fact.

—*Joe Ellefson*
online criminal justice instructor
Bismarck State College, North Dakota

learning principles, classes should be limited to manageable numbers for faculty.

The Precourse Letter

In the ideal world, a Web-based course should close for registration several weeks before it is to begin, and the faculty member should be provided with a list of e-mail and standard mailing addresses. In the real world, you should reasonably expect regular updates on enrollees that provide this information, preferably on a daily basis. If your institution is not providing these rosters, ask them to. It will greatly improve stu-

dents' satisfaction with online instruction, and everyone will benefit. Because well-taught online courses have a tendency to fill quickly, faculty can often have a fair amount of lead time to prepare students for the opening session.

We have already stressed the critical necessity for a well-developed online orientation, so we will assume that students are enrolling with the proper equipment and with a basic knowledge of how the platform used by the institution works. You as the instructor now have the opportunity to prepare your students with the information and tools needed to begin learning in your specific course on the opening day, without a barrage of e-mail and phone calls that consume time and heighten the frustration of the first week.

One of the most effective tools for this introduction is a letter and e-mail to each student. Because they may not be checking their college e-mail accounts regularly before the beginning of the term and may not be at the home address listed on a roster, attempts to reach students through both e-mail and regular postal service increase the odds of success. It takes only a few moments per student to generate a prewritten e-mail and letter and, if properly organized, it saves hours of work later.

This opening message provides an opportunity to personally welcome students and review first steps. Even Web-savvy students often are unclear about when and how an online class begins (no "Monday 10:00, Rm. L 101" on the schedule). Your letter should announce the first day of participation and express an expectation that students will log into the class on that date. Detailed, step-by-step instructions on how to get to the Web site and log in are critical. You should assume that every student in the class is taking a Web-based course for the first time. Indicate that when students reach the course Web site, another detailed message will be waiting, explaining what to do next. This may appear unnecessarily laborious and repetitive, but when you consider the trepidation with which a new community college student enters a building for the first time, tries to find the right classroom, and sits expectantly waiting to see if he or she has ended up in the right place, you begin to understand the potential anxiety. Your students are coming to a class with no room, no starting hour, and no one else sitting in the room to ask "is this the right place?"

Also use this letter to explain ways in which students can acquire the needed texts, course packs, or other materials you expect them to have in the first few weeks. Otherwise, you will face frustrating and wasteful delays as students claim not to be able to participate in discussion or complete assignments because they do not have a book. Online booksellers are convenient to students who live some distance from the bookstore, and they usually underprice college stores. Before suggesting specific online vendors, check to ensure that your choice is available and what the price ranges are for new and used editions.

You also should take the opportunity in this letter to explain whether your course will require anything beyond the standard equipment discussed in the orientation or in the college's general descriptive material about online courses. For example, if you are using video and students will need the hardware and software required to play a DVD, they will want access to something other than a slow dialup connection to download video clips. Explain this in the letter and suggest options such as an area library or college lab where computers will have DVD players and fast connections. You might also have the film clips available on CDs and ask students to let you know early if they anticipate equipment trouble. This will allow you to get the needed materials to students before an issue crops up.

The precourse message is an excellent opportunity to let students know how you will be corresponding with them during the term. Remind them to check college e-mail addresses daily if that is to be the primary mode of communication. A sample letter for an upcoming world religions course appears in appendix A. The e-mail follow-up reinforces the major points of the letter and attaches the syllabus as promised.

These initial messages begin to create as sense of learning community. You can tell students a little about yourself and express how excited you are to have them in class. Let them know that you are confident in their

success, if they commit the time and effort asked for in the syllabus. The letter essentially takes the place of the traditional first class session in which you go through the syllabus, review the texts, and describe how the class will operate. It allows you to begin your first class session by getting right into the course material.

Resources for Exploring Online Teaching

The Chronicle of Higher Education: Information Technology
http://chronicle.com/distance

KAIROS
http://english.ttu.edu/kairos
—a journal exploring the intersections of rhetoric, technology, and pedagogy

Learn the Net.com
www.learnthenet.com/english/index.html

Course Design

The ability to move quickly into the course depends, to a large degree, on a well-developed syllabus. A good syllabus is a reflection of a well-designed course. One of the values many instructors find in moving into the online environment is that it forces them to reexamine courses they have been teaching for years but have not continued to evaluate for currency, accommodation to new learning strategies, and use of the multitude of resources now available. We do not want to take much time here reviewing the elements of course design other than to suggest that development or conversion of your course for online delivery is an ideal time for that review. You might identify these elements by asking the following questions:

- What are the key learning objectives? When the course is over, what will I want students to know, and what skills will I want them to be able to demonstrate?
- With those learning objectives in mind, what will be the most useful resources for students to use

to acquire the essential information needed? Texts, course packs, supplemental readings, Web resources, activities, experiments?

- What will be the most successful processes for acquiring the knowledge and skills I want students to obtain? Lecture? Video or audio presentations? Web searches? Class discussion? Group work and collaborative projects?
- What are my own instructional strengths and weaknesses? How do they match the learning strategies that will be the most successful? Where they do not match, how can I gain the needed skills or tap the skills of others to make the most effective strategies available to my class?
- Given the teaching and learning format I am using, what assets and obstacles do I have that facilitate or impede reaching my objectives? How can I remove or compensate for the obstacle?
- What will be the most useful evaluation strategies and assessment tools for the class? How can I incorporate them into the delivery environment I will use?

Answering these questions on paper will create an outline of the course objectives you desire and how you plan best to achieve them. Procedurally, you will then want to move to the course development steps outlined later in this chapter and in chapter 7, leaving creation of the syllabus until you have organized the course and

Teaching Tip

Storyboard your course before putting it online, and look at it from a student's perspective. Look at a visual arrangement and organize the online presentation so that navigation from one area to the next is simple. Include specific, clear directions in each folder or item so that students know exactly what you want them to do there.

—*Terri Langan*
instructional development and delivery
Fox Valley Technical College, Wisconsin

created learning units. Your introductory letter and announcement, however, should immediately refer students to your syllabus.

Syllabus

Most institutions or departments provide guidelines for a basic syllabus, directing faculty to include office hours, provide a course description, list texts to be used, cite basic course objectives, and the like. However, in an online course, taking extra care to develop a complete and easy-to-follow syllabus is the next critical step to helping students succeed and to saving precious time. In appendix A, we present an example of what we consider to be an effective syllabus for the online world religions course discussed in the letter mentioned previously, but we use one of the other online platforms.

Course Subdivisions

As the sample syllabus in appendix A suggests, there is great organizational value in breaking your course down into units that, in this case, have been labeled "seminars." (We use *seminars* because the word indicates that each unit is self-contained.) These units, modules, seminars, or whatever you choose to call them, provide students with a detailed look at the course a few weeks at a time and will be discussed in greater length in the next chapter. As noted earlier, research by Moore (1989), Saba (1988), and Wheeler (2002), indicates that for students in a distance environment, "dialogue and course structure" are critical ingredients in effecting a student's sense of belonging and of psychological distance. The richer and more personal the dialogue is and the more structured the course is, the greater the sense of connection the students have. By moving students smoothly from your introductory announcement, to the syllabus, to carefully organized units of instruction, you are able to maintain this sense of structure.

In a semester format with 15 or 16 weeks, a comfortable and manageable seminar or module might contain 3 or 4 weeks of work and assignments. Some faculty members modularize each week and provide students with a course map that shows how

Teaching Tip

Design content for multipurpose use when possible. Requirements for format of assignments and testing procedures may be the same for several courses and from one semester to another. Place content in modules that are labeled with names and due dates—not just numbers. Consider showing only the current material. Do not allow students to work ahead.

—*Jo Ann Armstrong*
online psychology and sociology instructor
Patrick Henry Community College, Virginia

units will progress, adding a sense of continuity. If you are constructing your course for the first time, it is helpful to establish your learning objectives; review the text, course pack, or resource materials; and then chart out and sequence the objectives by units, modules, or seminars. You can then sequence your material over the course of the term. Where are the natural divisions? How might you most naturally divide your leaning objectives into four or five units, modules, or seminars? When you have arranged this sequence, you will have the basic divisions for your class. These units essentially become like folders in a computer file, and you place in each folder all of the pertinent information related to that unit of instruction. The student can then go to the unit folder and immediately find everything needed to complete that seminar. Each of these units becomes something of a standalone instructional module, and your learning strategies may vary significantly from one seminar to another. Edith Shaked of Pima Community College suggested,

Create a calendar divided into modules/themes and not just dates. I can teach my class during 8 weeks, 5 weeks, 16 weeks, or 14 weeks. I keep the same number of modules, and I just change the dates. I send a short introduction of every module, with the starting date. At the end, there is a section,

REMINDER, where I remind students of tests or projects to submit, even if they are already mentioned in the calendar. (E. Shaked, personal communication, December 9, 2005)

Using Seminars

One of the benefits of this modularized approach to instruction is that it creates, over time, an expansive storehouse of units that you can plug into various courses as they become applicable. They position you to share seminars or modules with faculty teaching similar courses, borrow units from others, or insert (with permission) professionally prepared units that address specific course objectives.

William Draves, president of the Learning Resources Network (LERN), illustrated the value of this modularization with the example of a unit on "Jackie Robinson and the Color Barrier" (Draves, 2002), which might have applicability in a course on the history of baseball or on race relations and diversity. Similarly, a unit on Darwin and the evolution of biological sciences could be used in courses ranging from biology to anatomy and physiology, to generic physical sciences. In the sample agenda shown in appendix A, students are asked to read an essay by a member of the Eastern Shawnee tribe, with an option to view the essay as a video presentation. A unit built around several similar essays would fit

Teaching Tip

It's often difficult for the online course designer to spot her or his own organization and navigation flaws. Have a colleague or student preview your course and critique your organization. Or have your current students conduct a usability analysis of your course design as an assignment or for extra credit.

—*Jim Burns*
online English instructor
Mountain Empire Community College, Virginia

nicely into a U.S. history curriculum, Native American studies, or religious studies.

The flexibility to create and use modular curricula and introduce units that take advantage of this growing library of online resources should become more apparent as we focus on the specifics of course development. In chapter 7, we follow the student's next steps in your online classroom and review the tools that help you organize the course and help your students become fully engaged in learning from it.

Managing Your Course and Time

In this chapter, we discuss how to most effectively use the online format to maximize learning while managing instruction time. We encourage you to think of instruction differently, take advantage of Web resources, and resist the temptation simply to import the classroom into the computer. We review techniques for delivering effective online lectures, using student groups, taking advantage of Web links, and keeping online instruction from becoming overly time-consuming. We outline the basic tools available and review the advantages and disadvantages of each.

The common online instructional platforms such as WebCT and Blackboard are often referred to as course management systems, and for good reason. They provide online instructors with an array of tools that assist with both the structural and interpersonal aspects of creating a productive learning environment. Not all of these tools are critical to your teaching success, and we recommend that if you are new to online instruction, you begin simply. You can develop and deliver a very engaging and involved course without using all of them and will save the time that trying to use unfamiliar or complicated tools can usurp.

When you and your students initially enter your class site, you will find an announcement page and a menu bar along the side that looks something like the example shown on page 43, taken from the Blackboard menu. WebCT uses a similar menu that can be modified by the instructor and commonly shows icons that

represent the tools the instructor has chosen to display on the home page.

The box just below the main menu appears only on the instructor's screen; by choosing Course Map or Control Panel, you may go to any of the choices mentioned and enter, modify, or delete information to build and manage the course. Although it may not be displayed in exactly this format, each course management instructor's home page will have a control panel selection that will allow you to manage and change course content. We will review the basic tools in this chapter in the order in which students are likely to use them, beginning with the moment a new student enters your classroom and sees your announcements.

Making the Best Use of Announcements

Each of the course management systems has an announcements section that generally fills a portion of the screen on the master menu when a student first enters. Using announcements as a regular communication tool provides a venue through which you can pass along general information and give instructions without having to create individual messages. We will not go into detail here about how to create an announcement, because the mechanics will vary from one platform to another. It is a straightforward process initiated through the faculty control panel and can be mastered quickly. Instead, we will focus on content.

Your initial announcement might look something like that in Figure 7.1. This announcement example is lengthy and may appear to be overly detailed. However, it takes the place, along with the letter you sent out initially, of the opening classroom

Figure 7.1. Example of a course announcement.

Welcome to Art History! Because you have reached this announcement, you have successfully been able to enter the course site and are ready to get started. Your first assignments are due Wednesday, August 21st, and, if you follow the steps below, you should be able to begin without difficulty. Now, please do the following to get under way:

1. Select Syllabus from the main menu. This takes you to a site where you will find the syllabus. Read the syllabus through completely! It will provide a good overview of the course, answer most of your questions, and save you time later. I suggest that you print a copy and keep it where you can refer to it. Then return back here or use the link at the end of the syllabus to go to Course Content.

2. Now select Course Content from the menu. This site contains a series of menu choices that break the course down into units of several weeks, called seminars. These include outlines for each week of the course. I will have only one seminar in view at a time in the Course Content section. Seminar 1 is waiting there for you. Open the Seminar 1 folder and find Agenda. It should be the first file and will tell you all you need to know to do your assignments, participate in discussion,

and meet assignment deadlines for the next few weeks. Print a copy of the agenda for each seminar and keep it as a handy reference. Once you have found your way to the Seminar 1 folder, reviewed the agenda, and looked over the rest of that folder's contents, come back to this page and read the rest of this announcement or select the link that takes you to the calendar.

3. Select Calendar on the main menu and look over how the course will progress. Note that key assignment dates are listed.

You can see now from the way each seminar is organized and from the calendar that knowing what is expected in the course will be a simple task. Always check this announcement site when you log in, and I will put any updates here. We also will be talking to each other each week on the discussion board.

Now, one last starting assignment. Return to Course Content and read through the file called "How I use WebCT." This will give you detailed instructions on how to access and use the parts of this Web site that I plan to use in the course. I suggest you look at this section even if you have had an online course before, because I may use some tools differently than other faculty. Again, welcome to Art History. I look forward to working with you this semester!

session in which you review syllabus, discuss classroom procedures, and address introductory questions. To the extent you can anticipate questions, and answer them through this announcement, you will not be answering them one-by-one via e-mail.

Course Information

Your first referenced site was the Syllabus file. This site may have other names with different course management systems. The syllabus generally is placed under Course Information in the Blackboard system, for example. In some area connected to the main menu, you will want to create a location or locations for generic information about the course—material that is not session or assignment specific. This would be an ideal place to locate the following:

- The course syllabus
- A detailed review of how you use the course manager (see "How to Use Blackboard" in appendix A)
- Sample paper or project formats
- Other information students will need (that should always be visible)

If you use the organizational system we suggest, your seminar or unit folders will appear and disappear as you approach and complete units of instruction. Therefore, you need a location for information that always can be accessed. Course Information or Course Content can provide that location. In your calendar or agenda for each seminar, as you list assignments where aids found in this course information area might be helpful (i.e., sample papers), a brief reference note or link can send students to this location.

Course Documents

We have chosen to place our seminar folders in the Course Documents or Course Content section of the course manager, although some faculty choose to use the Assignments section for this purpose. When directed to this section by your introductory announcement, students should immediately see your Seminar or Unit

Blackboard Menu

Announcements	Communication
Course Information	Discussion Board
Staff Information	External Links
Course Documents	Tools
Assignments	Control Panel

1 folder and, on opening the folder, find the top item to be the seminar calendar or agenda.

Agendas

For each seminar, it is important to create a week-by-week calendar or agenda that provides detailed instructions about everything expected for each week of the seminar. This should include reading assignments, instructions on how to get to lectures and supplemental readings, discussion questions, due dates, upcoming assignments, and the like. We recommend using an agenda even if you use the course calendar tool. The calendar functions generally do not allow convenient space to display all of the information you will want to include on your agenda. A sample agenda for Seminar 1, which in this case contains the first 2 weeks of the world religions course used earlier as an illustration, appears in appendix A, page 134. This brief introductory seminar allows students to become familiar with the online format and to experiment with the course management system before being overwhelmed with assignments.

This sample agenda covers only 2 weeks, whereas a typical module or seminar will generally cover 3 or 4 weeks, but it displays the essential ingredients. Through this agenda, students are provided with the following:

- Learning objectives
- A step-by-step outline of what is expected to achieve the objectives
- Due dates for each assignment
- A detailed list of the resources to use and where to look for supplemental material if students wish to do additional exploration

Teaching Tip

Discussion board postings can be time-consuming for the instructor to read, evaluate, and respond to. When using a course management system such as WebCT or Blackboard, compile discussion postings into a single text file that covers one or more days, then print, read off line, and write your responses in the margins. Replies are generally more concise, and multiple instances of the same question can be addressed in one posting from the instructor.

—Francine Van Meter
distance education coordinator
Cabrillo College, California

- A description of how you expect them to get information to you and other class members
- A review of the learning approaches you plan to use: short written lectures, readings, Net pals, Web searches, external links, video clips, and threaded discussion
- Instructions on how to find procedural information related to each and a description of what you expect, to grant full credit for discussion and written responses

This first agenda, in addition to outlining the assignments for the beginning weeks, provides students with the opportunity to

- Use the discussion board
- Send e-mail to you and to the rest of the class using the platform's e-mail list
- Complete a search on the Web
- Use the External Links feature of this particular platform
- View an imbedded video clip if their equipment allows

Most of the tools used during the semester are introduced to the students in these first sessions.

Note that much of the information on the agenda repeats what the introductory announcement contained and what students found in the syllabus. Remember, repetition is one of the key elements in controlling your time. Marty Hill, Coordinator of the Virtual Campus at New Mexico's San Juan Community College, noted

One of the most important things an online instructor can do to assist their students (especially in intro courses) is to provide lots of redundancy when it comes to navigation and information. For example, a due date might be mentioned in a message box on the course home page, in the calendar, on the course timeline, in a discussion posting and even an e-mail. Likewise, you can provide a link to quizzes as a graphic icon on the homepage, in the course menu, within a content module and from the calendar. Most course management systems make it very easy to establish a pattern of redundancy. Using redundancy will save an instructor many e-mails detailing navigation trails to lost students. As students become more accustomed to your course, you can survey them to find out which cue locations are most helpful. (M. Hill, personal communication, December 9, 2005)

The syllabus and agendas are the points at which you begin this redundancy by repeating, linking, emphasizing, and highlighting. As we turn now to the creation of specific instructional tools, this pattern of reiteration will remain a theme.

Incorporating Learning Principles

Within each unit or seminar there are any number of ways to organize student activities; however, some general pedagogical principles, if applied to the organization of your units, can both improve learning and assist with time management. Before discussing specific assignments and exercises that work well in the online environment, a brief review of basic learning principles will be especially helpful to new faculty and to those examining their courses for delivery in a new format.

Chickering and Gamson's (1987) "seven principles for good practice in undergraduate education" are commonly referenced for creating an effective learning environment. They should be reviewed when any course is developed or modified:

1. Good practice encourages student–faculty contact.
2. Good practice encourages cooperation among students.
3. Good practice encourages active learning.
4. Good practice gives prompt feedback.
5. Good practice emphasizes time on task.
6. Good practice communicates high expectations.
7. Good practice respects diverse talents and ways of knowing. (Chickering & Gamson, 1987)

The online learning environment lends itself to these principles as naturally as does the traditional classroom. But although these seven principles apply to all learning situations, the means by which they are incorporated may vary depending on the nature of the community of learners. How, for example, does one best encourage cooperation and active learning among adults who have been out of school for a decade?

Over the past 30 years, a philosophical debate has been raging between scholars in adult education and the rest of the academic community about whether the term *pedagogy* can appropriately be applied to all stages and ages involved in learning. Adult educators contend that adults learn quite differently than do children—the group to whom the term pedagogy was initially applied. Malcomb Knowles, one of the early pioneers in adult learning, pointed out that the term is a combination of the Greek words for *child* and *leading*. Pedagogy generally refers to the art and science of how children learn (cited in Gehring, 2000, p. 151).

In a compendium by Gehring of research on what adult learning specialists label *andragogy,* Knowles is further quoted as identifying four assumptions of

> **Teaching Tip**
>
> Avoid assigning busy work and instead focus students on doing a variety of tasks for each week, such as having students read the material and then discussing it in a chat room or threaded discussion.
> —*Jaclyn Allen*
> *online English instructor*
> *Bismarck State College, North Dakota*

adult learning that differentiate it from children's learning and serve to define andragogy:

1. Moves in self-concept from being a dependent personality toward being self-directed
2. Accumulates a reservoir of experience that serves as a learning resource
3. Defines readiness to learn more specifically in terms of the developmental tasks related to social roles.
4. Sees more immediate application of knowledge and therefore sees learning as being more problem-centered than subject centered (cited in Gehring, 2000, p. 157)

Based on these four assumptions, Bangura (2003) noted that teachers can expect adult students to be more autonomous learners, to rely more on experience in making judgments about both content and relevance, to wish to be more actively involved in determining their learning needs, and to want the learning to have immediate value.

These distinctions become particularly important to community college faculty who are aware that the differences between pedagogical and andragogical characteristics are less a matter of chronological age than of maturity and status. A 30-year old community college freshman with high developmental needs may retain a very dependent personality, have a limited reservoir of experiential knowledge, and have such a poor sense of future possibilities that he or she is not concerned about immediate applicability of learning. This student falls into the description of pedagogy as completely as does a normal eighth grader. Yet in the same course, you might have a 25-year-old Gulf War veteran with an undergraduate degree in biology, who has returned to the community college to acquire certification in fire science. As an instructor, you must therefore be prepared to facilitate both andragogy and pedagogy in your approach.

Traditional instruction has largely been designed for and directed at pedagogic learners. Gehring recommended a number of strategies that must be added to a teacher's bag of instructional tools if one is to effectively accommodate the adult learner:

- Remove the accoutrements of childishness from the learning environment.
- To the degree possible, allow the learner to help define his or her learning needs.
- Provide as much input as possible into the planning of the learning process.
- Present the learning process as one of mutual teacher–learner responsibility.
- Emphasize experiential techniques.
- Demonstrate where possible, practical application for that being learned. (Gehring, 2000)

Drawing on the work of a number of recent scholars in learning theory—such as Bruffee, Matthews, and Whipple—Cross (1999) suggested that we are entering an age when it no longer can be assumed that learning is a matter of gaining access to and grasping knowledge that exists somewhere out there. Learning may instead be something that we construct through interactions with the information that exists in a field, with others who have worthwhile perspectives about that information, and with the environment in which the learning is occurring. The role of the teacher in this learning approach becomes one of exploring with the students, not as a giver of knowledge, but as a mentor in identifying useful resources.

Referring back to our earlier discussion of the requirements of students with developmental issues, we can see that this open approach to exploration

Teaching Tip

Just as in the traditional classroom, use deadlines. Be very specific. If you want an assignment in and complete by Sunday, 12/18/05 at 3:00 pm Central time, tell students exactly that and specify what happens if it is late or improperly posted or submitted (e.g., a penalty or not accepted for grading). You want the students to get things done and in on time, right? Well, they want to know how they did. Get a response to them within a reasonable period of time. This obviously will depend on what the assignment was. Just don't make them wait until the end of the semester to find out how they did on the first test.

—*Joe Ellefson*
online criminal justice instructor
Bismarck State College, North Dakota

becomes particularly challenging to students who need highly structured environments and who expect the teacher to be the provider of knowledge. Online instruction may, in many ways, make facilitating the needs of these diverse learners less daunting than in the on-ground classroom.

Using Lecture as a Learning Catalyst

These lessons in effectiveness do not mean that we must abandon all traditional approaches to instruction. Cross noted that students must still experience a series of interactions with the scholarly foundations that exist in a field, and there is nothing wrong with providing a well-developed presentation or with requiring regular reading from applicable texts. Andragogy simply encourages attention to applicability and relevance and provides an opportunity for students to become actively involved in the learning process.

The direction in text development in recent years has been toward increased use of examples, case studies, and "applied" discussion. Teachers preparing online courses that include a mix of adult students will benefit from reviewing new texts or course packs in the discipline to see what is available. But regular reading assignments and a short written or recorded lecture can respond to adult learners' needs by adding context and demonstrating applicability, and they can be excellent ways to structure a week for less mature learners. They also can provide the basis for engaging in dialogue and sharing relevant experience.

Appendix A contains a brief lecture example from a business or leadership course that accompanies a reading assignment about ethics (see page 137). The example illustrates how the lecture can be used to complement the text, introduce relevant supplemental material, and establish a basis for engaging students in dialogue on the discussion board. We use this lecture as the basis for several of the other illustrations provided later in the book. Please read the lecture before continuing, because it serves as the basis for the next several paragraphs.

The sample lecture is relatively short—three or four typed pages. In addition to complementing the reading students have done during the week, it uses a number of the elements important to adults, millennials, and less mature learners. It invites immediate application to the lives of the students, asking that they consider dilemmas in their own situations that illustrate points being raised. It sends them, if interested, onto the Web to find material that complements or clarifies the subject and instructs them to use video as part of the learning process for the coming week. The use of case studies and "give examples from your experience" questions provide immediate applicability and invite a degree of personal disclosure by students. This strategy will aid in building a sense of community among the learners—a goal that is assisted by the instructor's willingness to share personal thoughts of his or her own. The teacher reminds students that they have a live chat or synchronous chat session scheduled for the following Wednesday and tells them what they need to have prepared. The lecture also indicates what must be in the Seminar 2 folder in Course Documents or Course Content to support this session:

- The lecture
- The excerpt from Burns's writing
- The film clip from "Enron"
- The Hannan and Welch Case

The lecture also allows students to click directly to linked Web sites and gives explicit instructions for posting answers to the discussion board. With this information and what is provided in the agenda for this week, students know exactly what to do and when to do it. Yet they are provided with the freedom and encouragement to seek information elsewhere and to apply what they have learned from their own experience to the session.

Some online faculty members choose to put online lectures in a video or PowerPoint format, allowing them to create visuals that support the themes of the lecture and, if they wish, use embedded audio and video. It is now a relatively simple matter to videotape or audiotape a personal presentation and place it in the Seminar folder for students to watch. Remember here again, though, that it is important not to require too much of the students' hardware and software unless you know that they have the capabilities. Otherwise, you will be spending an inordinate amount of time preparing them for the course or addressing questions once under way. For this reason, lectures put on video also might be posted in text form for those with limited video capability.

Short lectures, especially when supplemental to other reading or research, provide an excellent catalyst for discussion and, in the case of this example, lead students directly to a chat session and to the discussion board. Because stimulating an engaging online discussion is so critical to the success of Web-based courses, we dedicate the next chapter to discussion and collaborative exercises and continue here with a review of other assignment choices and course management tools.

Building Learning Community Through Assignments

The choice of weekly assignments can add the variety needed to appeal to and accommodate the wide spectrum of learners you can expect in community college courses. These assignments also allow you to take full advantage of the flexibility and creative tools afforded by immediate access to the Web. Assignments might, for example, include Web searches that challenge students to follow a chain of discovery initiated by a series of questions. You also can arrange for an e-mail or synchronous chat discussion with a prominent authority in the area being reviewed. A Web search can be combined with a scheduled chat, sending students out to look for resources while engaged in a live spontaneous discussion. (For a useful resource in developing or using Web searches, see www.webquest.org.)

Using our world religions course as an example, students might be asked to go onto the Web and find as much information as they can about the pre-Aryan inhabitants of the Indus River Valley who inhabited the ancient cities of Harrappa and Mohenjo Daro. This could be done asynchronously or during a coordinated live chat session in which they exchange information about sites as they find them. After this exploration, arrangements could be made to put the class in touch with an archeologist at a Pakistani university to discuss what the most recent findings are telling us about this mysterious people and their contributions to early Hindu thought. If approached with sufficient time, specialists are often willing to commit an hour to a synchronous chat session, participate as a guest in a forum on the discussion board for a few days, or address e-mail questions submitted by students.

Another example is a project for which students demonstrate an understanding of a specific period in art's historic development. (The guidelines for the project appear in appendix A, page 141.) This assignment incorporates many of the elements of effective learning discussed previously and builds technological skills while doing so. It allows the learner to help define his or her learning needs and to have as much input as possible into the planning of the learning process. It emphasizes experiential techniques and suggests some application for that being learned. It allows students to teach each other and could easily be modified to make the assignment

collaborative, with dyads or small groups creating the projects. Students are directed to resources contained in the Seminar folder that can teach them skills they may not already possess for creating an illustrated document. They are now ready to share this assignment with each other.

Posting and Exchanging Documents

Before describing a number of the useful course management tools, we need to emphasize a simple principle about developing and organizing your lectures and assignments: You do not need to create your course using the course management system. Virtually all of the development can be done on your computer hard drive in a series of file folders that replicate your modules or seminars. Create lectures, assignments, readings, video clips, and the like in these folders, then copy them to the place you want them in your online course. Ideally, video clips can be placed on a central computer media server for your college, where they can then be streamed to your students' computers, saving the storage space and download problems of large files. Streaming video is discussed at greater length in chapter 9.

When you select Course Documents or Course Content on your Control Panel menu, for example, you will see a tool bar that invites you to add a file, create a folder, add a course link, and so forth. By selecting these choices, you can name the new file, then select a browse command that allows you to go to your personal folders and copy any of your created materials to your online course folders. The major course management platforms then provide a number of tools for viewing, posting, and exchanging materials and assignments, and these tools have improved in simplicity and flexibility over the years. One of the earliest was what is commonly referred to as the "digital drop box," but this has now been replaced in the Blackboard system with the Assignment Manager.

A simple means of exchanging documents is as e-mail attachments. This method allows students and instructors to share text documents, spreadsheets, photo files, and presentations in formats such as

PowerPoint with relative ease. There will be a feature in most course management systems that allows you and students to send e-mail to class members, selected groups, or to the entire class. E-mail does present several drawbacks, however, and you will benefit from becoming familiar with other assignment exchange tools available in the course management system.

E-mail is not always secure, and when graded assignments are being exchanged that include performance and student identification information, e-mail should be avoided. In addition, once e-mail becomes the standard method of exchange, students often begin to send material using their personal e-mail addresses rather than the address provided by the platform. College information systems that use security filters, spam control, file length limitations, and other restrictions on incoming mail will occasionally filter out attachments that are not seen by the filters as adhering to guidelines. Student work can be stopped before it reaches you. By avoiding e-mail as the transmission vehicle, you avoid both the student confidentiality issues and the "I know I sent that to you . . . I don't know why you didn't get it" debates that this method can create.

Fortunately, with each of the major course management systems, better options do exist. Blackboard, for example, has designed its Assignment Manager to allow you to post assignments, exchange documents confidentially, and automatically create an entry in the grade book for the project. Students know where to look for their work and receive your comments on it just as they would if it were attached to an e-mail. The most effective way to learn to use these tools is to explore the content areas in your course management system, then practice sending files back and forth with a colleague.

Calendar

The major course management systems provide a calendar function that allows you to enter activities so that they can be viewed a day, week, or month at a time. These calendars are especially useful for providing students with a broad general timeline for the

> ### Teaching Tip
>
> Having all assignments for a testing period available at the beginning of the testing period enables the student to know what is expected by the time the next test is due. Do not make the entire course available from the beginning, however, because it may overwhelm the student and takes away some flexibility in varying content. Monitor the course daily or every other day with your own personal deadlines for course maintenance. Answer students' e-mails daily or within 24 hours except on the weekends. Organize all modules in the same way so that students become familiar with the layout.
>
> —*Jo Ann Armstrong*
> *online psychology and sociology instructor*
> *Patrick Henry Community College, Virginia*

course and for highlighting key assignment deadlines, breaks, and holidays. These calendaring functions are also easy to learn and simple to construct and modify. We find that supplementing the calendar with much more detailed agendas for each unit or seminar saves a great deal of time and avoids numerous questions and e-mails.

Creating a Grade Book

Establishing a grade book in your course management system will take an hour of time before the course begins, but it will save you that hour many times over once in place. To use the hour most effectively,

- Make a list on paper of your graded assignments in the order you plan to use them.
- Determine how the grade will be awarded (e.g., points, letter grade, complete/incomplete).
- Establish a due date.
- Go to the grade book site on your course management platform menu and follow what are fairly simple instructions for entering assignments. (The Assignment Manager in Black-

Teaching Tip

The weeks in my class run from Monday to Sunday, but typically I will give students access to the next week on the Thursday before. That way, if necessary, they have two weekends for the assignments and can better plan their workload. If the material and assignments are related, of course, I give access to more than 1 week at a time.

—*Jane Schreck*
online English instructor
Bismarck State College, North Dakota

board enables you to place an entry in the grade book as you create the assignment.)

There are a number of good reasons for using this efficient grade book tool. In addition to serving the purposes of the traditional grade book, the online version generally keeps running point totals for each student. It also allows you to look at any student's grade or assignment at a glance, determine completion information, and perform other statistical reviews that can be extremely helpful to course management and improvement.

These grade book statistical functions, for obvious reasons, best lend themselves to point-based grading. If you have been using letter grades, it may be beneficial to assign these grades a numerical value. The grade book also allows students to examine their own progress and question entries as they appear, rather than at the end of the term.

The grade book function is especially useful for encouraging and tracking work on the discussion board. Initial responses to instructors' questions, for example, can be assigned a point value, as can responses to other students' postings. As you describe in the syllabus what you expect from a good response, you can give numerical values to partial, weak, or late responses in your description (e.g., "You will receive no more than 5 of the 10 points if you do not reference the text or lecture material in

your answer.") As you post points for responses, students know immediately when they are not meeting expectations by a reduction in points.

Other Tools

The course management tools reviewed to this point in the book are sufficient to organize and deliver a very effective online course. They will give you what you need to systematize your materials, keep students informed, exchange assignments, and keep grade reports. Chapter 8 expands on the use of the discussion feature. In chapter 12 we review various assessment techniques and discuss testing and measurement tools built into the platforms—a final essential course element. Each platform also provides a menu of other useful tools, although these begin to move into the realm of "extras," and you can introduce them into your course management as time and interest allow.

Virtual Classroom/Whiteboard and Chat enable you to arrange for simultaneous discussion or chat sessions with your class. The virtual classroom or whiteboard feature provides the use of writing tools visible to all during synchronous sessions, much as you would use them in the traditional course. Our experience has been that these synchronous tools are most useful for small classes and smaller group work, in part because it is difficult to get a full class together at a specific time, and in

Teaching Tip

Establish office hours so that your online students know when they can reach you rather than leave a message. I check my e-mail daily to see whether students are having problems with an assignment. I usually let students know on my home page that I will get back to them within 24 hours unless it's a holiday or weekend, and I stick to that.

—*Therese Millis*
online physical therapy instructor
San Juan College, New Mexico

part because large group involvement in a synchronous exercise limits participation, and students have a difficult time remaining engaged. The virtual classroom is useful for the entire class in situations in which the class is small or when the main purpose is demonstration, such as in a math course when the instructor wishes to work through a set of sample problems in a forum in which all can see the work and ask questions as they arise.

The Group functions in the course management systems allow the instructor to create subgroups that have the same opportunities to exchange e-mail and information, conduct chats, and hold discussions or virtual classroom sessions that are available only to the assigned group. These features become particularly important as you introduce collaborative exercises and want to permit private group discussion and exchange.

Course Options

A group of tools also exists that allows you to copy your course, archive it, import packages from other courses, or export your course for use by others. We recommend that you contact your system administrator and discuss these tools before using them. System administrators often prefer to control these tools to maintain continuity in course archiving and activation, and they may save you considerable time by assisting with these functions. The institution should make guidelines for the use of these tools part of your faculty online orientation program.

Teaching Tip

No busy work! Assign activities that will allow students to show what they are reading and exploring and to perform skills you need to see them perform. Keep all work at the level of rigor expected in a traditional classroom. Keep multimedia simple and easy to download and run. Use learning objects; students love them.

—*Terri Langan*
instructional development and delivery
Fox Valley Technical College, Wisconsin

Most of us learned to use computers through a combination of instruction or personal tutoring, followed by practice and experimentation. We retain those skills that we use on a regular basis and have to be refreshed on those we do not. You will find this to be the case with the course management tools. Those you use frequently will become second nature. Those you use occasionally will require regular review. Each system includes on its main menu a well-indexed manual that addresses virtually any question, and as we constantly remind students, "There are no foolish questions." Practice, explore, experiment, and ask others, and you will find that this array of tools will allow you to open the world of learning to your students in ways that have never been possible in the past.

CHAPTER 8

Facilitating Discussion and Collaborative Exercises

In this chapter, we focus on the use of various active learning strategies—from stimulating online dialogue to involving students in collaborative activities and group exercises.

The lecture example and project assignment discussed in chapter 7 and appendix A both require students to participate in what is called a threaded discussion on the discussion board. The discussion board in all of the platforms allows the instructor to create a forum in which threads of discussion develop around a topic. The participant initiating the thread introduces the theme, and others respond to that entry by selecting a reply choice. The mechanics are quite simple and easy to learn, but they should be explained to students in detail either in the syllabus, the first agenda, or a separate file in the Seminar 1 folder.

Threaded Discussion

When you first begin discussions on the discussion board, initial responses will probably be something like the following examples from the art history class we have been using as one of our illustrations. Shawn started this thread with her response to the first assignment question:

The sarcophagus: The sarcophagus really was a neat statue to me. It really is the first figure that shows a couple that might indeed love each other or stand to be near each other. For some reason you are just drawn into this figure for some reason. The flow of the statue seems to me like it is a bed that they are laying on and the couple is in an intimate moment.

Other than the fact that they are staring into space liekt hey [sic] are posing for a picture. I wonder if it is a portrait of a couple and if they really did pose for an artist???

Kelly: I also like the couple. It is nice to see them act as if they really love each other not just a required kind of thing. I also wondered if the people pose for the statues or if the artist just did it from memory.

Betsy: You're right. It is like the first statue that shows a couple in love. It is awkward how they are staring into space, as if posed.

Through your instructions, reminders, coaching, and grading of these responses during the first few weeks, you should be able to help students move toward a more sophisticated level of dialogue as reflected in this later response in the same course. Here is a response from Carol:

The Hildesheim Column: I found the bronze spiral column with reliefs, illustrating the life of Christ (figure 16–25) especially interesting. This is an item that Bishop Bernward had cast for his new church in Hildesheim, Germany. As the book says, it was probably begun sometime after the doors were set in place and completed before the Bishop's death in 1022. The seven spiral bands of the relief tell the story of Jesus' life in 24 scenes, beginning with his baptism and concluding with his entry into Jerusalem. These are the missing episodes from the story told on the cast bronze doors. The column resembles Trajan's in Rome, with the narrative reading from bottom to top, just like Trajan's. It is speculated that Trajan's column served as the model for this one, even though its narrative unfolds from right to left, instead of from left to right as on this one. How do they cast a huge column like that, do you think?

Over time, your goal is to encourage skills in dialogue that will lead to threaded discussion similar to that generated by the questions at the end of the sample lecture about ethics (see appendix A). The agenda instructed students to read the lecture, then go to the discussion board where a forum had already been created for their responses. Here are initial responses from Janice:

Legal but not ethical: It is legal to assist visitors from other countries who receive visas for specific reasons such as religious persecution, medical conditions or attend school. It is not ethical to arrange for these visas for true situations but once they are here, have them "pay you back" by being a nanny, maid or underpaid employee for a business. This situation relates to the guideline of mutuality (text, p. 218).

Teaching Tip

At the beginning of each course, we examine etiquette for both e-mail and discussion board. I have students read an article on e-mail etiquette, then send a note to the entire class commenting on what they have learned and practicing their own e-mail etiquette. Each bulletin board opens with a set of guidelines for communicating in that arena. Both help create a respectful online environment.

—Chris Rubio
online English instructor
American River College, California

Teaching Tip

I build the primary question based on the topic discussion area. Then I try to get out of the way of the students. (Some people, as in the traditional classroom, are intimidated by the presence or the scrutiny of the instructor). I observe and monitor and make adjustments if students stray a little in their interpretations or views of the content. I make it a point to never criticize or cut down an input in the online discussion. I may make several "adjustments" or perhaps "suggest" another perspective. I don't want to lose any student as a willing participant. Then in the grading portion, where there is one-on-one interaction, I may make a specific correction or note to a student.

—Joe Ellefson
online criminal justice instructor
Bismarck State College, North Dakota

The sponsor and the person sponsored are not working under the same set of rules and understandings.

Ethical but not legal: A businessman employs documented alien workers. It is a small, tight-knit group of the same men who return every year. The alien workers become like a second family to the businessman. One alien has become very close to the businessman serving as an interpreter and helping the work become even more productive. The alien asks the businessman if he can bring his wife who he misses very much during the long months in the Unites States. The businessman suspects the wife will be undocumented but he values the work of his "foreman" and does not want to lose him. He also wants the man to be happy in the United States. He agrees without asking questions.

Rachael: I think your Ethical but not Legal example really shows the complexity of these issues. The businessman really wanted to show his gratitude toward one of the alien workers by allowing his wife to come into the U.S. even though she would most likely be undocumented. I wonder how this meets the ethical criteria listed under Number 4 in the lecture though—about the action showing genuine concern for the legitimate interests of others. Is the businessman thinking about other workers who might be displaced by lower paid illegals, like the wife, if she works? There are both pros and cons on each side of the coin. Both the ethical and the legal choice pose risks like in your example but it has to be more than just what "feels right."

Dave: Janice, I'll be curious to see how people react about the ethics of the "undocumented" issue. It raises all kinds of questions about why we have immigration law, whether we should exercise it (or wink at it) differently based on nationality, whether a law can be a good and bad one at the same time, etc. Should I stop for stop lights at 3:00 a.m. at night when I am the only car on the road and I can see for blocks in all directions—especially when I'm driving in an area I know is crime ridden?

LaPonda: Legally you should stop at the red light at 3:00 am. But I would not recommend it. My mother lives on the corner of Jones and Donnelly. There are all sorts of illegal activity that goes on around there. I would rather get a ticket for running a red light than to get car jacked. I never stop at the light at the corner when it gets late. Another example is my sister she lives at the corner of Davis and Goodland. This is a drug infested area known for its gang affiliation called Bloods. All the streets surrounding Davis have stop signs and are one ways. I never stop at the stop signs in the day time or at night. Is this wrong? or Safe? So I guess legally it is wrong but ethically, I feel it is right.

Janice: I see this as being different from the red light decision. The issues of undocumented aliens in our country is the big problem no one wants to address. It is not an easy topic but it is timely and necessary. Changes in the economy will bring it to a forefront. The discussion will disappear but the individuals will not. For all concerned, dialogue must be initiated and worked on at the federal level. I am curious if anyone else has an opinion they will share.

Instructor: How do the rest of you feel about this? The "red light" and "illegal immigrant" situations are both good examples of cases that might be ethical but not legal. But how do they stand up to all four of Burn's criteria and Kidder's dyads?

This set of responses came from a class of older adult students and is the kind of dialogue you want to develop as the term progresses. Note that in the initial response, Janice follows the instruction to reference a point in the reading material, and Rachael also points to a principle presented in the lecture. This requirement that, at least in their initial postings, students must refer to the study materials keeps the threaded discussion from becoming no more than a list of expressed opinions.

Teaching Tip

In threaded discussions, it's all in the wording of the question. I also check in frequently to make sure no one is getting off track, particularly the first responders.
—Jane Schreck
online English instructor
Bismarck State College, North Dakota

Discussion will be greatly enriched by following a set of simple practices:

1. Provide an outline in your syllabus or in the first agenda of what you expect in an acceptable discussion response. For example: "To get full credit for a discussion entry, it must be a paragraph or two long; must reference the lecture, reading, or other resource material to support your points; and must be based on more than personal opinion."

2. Use your involvement as instructor primarily to keep discussion focused, moving forward, and constructive. You will find that when you offer your own views and observations, they are often taken as the final word and will bring the thread to a halt. Ask questions, provide summarizing assistance, but, to the greatest

degree possible, allow the students to manage the discussion. (See chapter 5, "Characteristics of Capable Teachers," for additional recommendations.)

3. Be firm with your scoring or grading of initial entries, and you will greatly improve the quality of discussion. If using point-based grading for entries, you might offer 10 points for a well-developed initial posting but let students know that unless they reference the text or lecture in the answer, it can receive no more than 5 points; then stick to it. It will take only one or two rounds of grading before students all begin to reference these resources. This will, of course, require immediate grading feedback.

4. Generate or borrow a brief review of discussion "netiquette"—a description of what is and is not appropriate in online dialogue. Place this in your Course Information section. Suggest in this review that your more experienced computer users avoid e-mail slang, abbreviations, and jargon, or you will spend unnecessary time explaining postings to other students and will receive entries such as "CUL8R" (See You Later!)". For a review of netiquette taken from Virginia Shea's book of the same title, see www.albion.com/netiquette.

5. Provide specific timelines by which discussion entries must be posted and responses given. For example, "You must reply to the postings of at least two of your classmates by 5:00 p.m. Friday to be considered for full credit."

6. Create on the discussion board a "sidebar" or "water cooler" forum and ask students to use this forum for social chat and for dialogue that does not pertain directly to the topic at hand. These are common names given to a forum that allows students to visit and socialize more casually, without adding to required reading for others. Remind early strays that they need to "please move to the Sidebar forum for this discussion," and it will begin to self-regulate.

7. Although a series of lecture- or assignment-based questions provides structure for your discussion, every now and then allow for more open-ended dialogue. At the end of a seminar unit, for example, you might invite students to comment on the lesson learned in that unit that has been the most personally meaningful and explain why. This open-ended discussion will encourage students to open up in ways that more structured questions do not allow and will add considerably to bringing the class together.

Framing Questions

Facilitating full and rich discussion depends to a large degree on your ability to frame questions well. You will need to experiment with question formulation and will get better at it over time. However, several principles will aid in developing questions that assist, rather than impede, good dialogue.

1. *Good discussion questions have more than one answer and afford more than one point of view.* A question in a psychology class that asks, "What are the steps in Maslow's Hierarchy of Needs?" is not a discussion question. Once a student has responded with the list of steps, there is not much need for other answers. A question might ask instead "How do the stages in Maslow's Hierarchy demonstrate differences between his humanistic approach and Freudian theory or behaviorism?" Now students have an opportunity to mention stages while comparing, contrasting, analyzing, and disagreeing.

2. *Questions should invite the use of higher-level thinking skills.* Benjamin Bloom's famous taxonomy suggested that different kinds of questions elicit different levels of cognitive processing, ranging from a basic reflection of knowledge, through comprehension, application, analysis, synthesis, and evaluation. To meet the requirements of Principle 1—that questions should allow for more than one answer—discussion questions must move beyond eliciting a basic expression of knowledge. To provide opportunities for active learning, they should engage students at several other levels of thinking. Question 2-4C at the end of the sample lecture on ethics in appendix A illustrates how the use of a case study invites thinking that includes application, analysis, synthesis, and evaluation. You will not, of course, receive responses of equal depth and insight from all students, but to the degree possible, some of your questions should allow for a full range of responses.

3. *Expect good answers and grade accordingly.* Chickering's and Gamson's 6th principle of good practice is that good practice communicates high expectation. So should your assessment of discussion responses. One of the unique values of online learning is that students must participate in discussion. The asynchronous nature of online dialogue allows every response to be a considered one and, as a teacher, you should expect no less. Many students comment that the discussion por-

Teaching Tip

Make discussions inviting, challenging, and worth getting online for, for all participants. Include probing questions, timely input yourself, lots of interaction, and humor. Require participation as part of successful completion requirements.

—Terri Langan
instructional development and delivery
Fox Valley Technical College, Wisconsin

tion of online classes is the area from which they learn the most—from each other. This will improve greatly if you insist from the beginning on thoughtful postings. One value of online course management systems is that they facilitate immediate grading feedback. By posting a point-based grade on entries within a few days after a discussion ends, you can remind students immediately of any quality concerns you have with their answers.

4. *For large classes, consider several sets of questions or several smaller groups responding to the same questions.* This recommendation does place an extra burden on the instructor. But students tire of having to think of new things to say when they are the 20th student to respond to your question. If classes are large, you can create several sets of questions, with subgroups responding to each set. Or smaller groups can respond to the same questions on their own discussion boards, keeping students from feeling as if there is nothing new to contribute. You also broaden the discussion and add new learning opportunities by using several question sets with smaller groups, but with all students able to read responses across all groups.

5. *While controlling your discussion participation, be careful not to be silent.* We cautioned earlier about the stifling effect instructors can have on discussion by offering opinions too often or too

definitively. Remaining absent can be equally damaging. Students want to know you are present and interested, and it is important to carefully time well-placed questions, observations, and related thoughts.

Collaborative Exercises

The dialogue among students becomes much more open and trusting as the students become better acquainted through various collaborative learning experiences. (You will occasionally hear people engage in heated debate about the difference between "cooperative" and "collaborative" learning, and we may upset some of the purists by using the terms interchangeably. Nevertheless, we are not going to worry about the distinction here.)

At first blush, involving students in group learning and collaboration in an online course appears daunting. But with a little time committed to group formation and to constructive group activities, online collaboration can prove to be a better learning experience than its traditional on-ground counterpart. The instructor of an online introduction to teaching course that had attracted enrollees from several states and from urban and rural communities commented, for example, that her class was enjoying some of the best collaborative work she had experienced because the online format allowed such enrollment diversity.

Conversely, there can be a fine line between useful group work and busy work. Students immediately recognize assignments that are superficial and that lack sound learning objectives. A number of collaborative learning exercise books and Web sites are available to faculty, and you need to sort through these carefully to find activities that have real substance. Many do exist, however, and you can create others by remodeling some of your favorite projects to turn them into group activities. Some of the most common active learning strategies that involve collaborative involvement include those described in the following sections.

Small-Group Work

This strategy falls into the category of the obvious, but is often poorly used. An effective example might be a case study in which each member of the group is asked to submit an initial, independent case analysis to group members, with a group assignment to then develop a collaborative or negotiated solution and recommendation. The value of the independent analysis is that it requires each group member to participate in initial input and provides the group with a variety of possibilities. Dominant group members then find it much more difficult to force a solution on the group, and reticent members find it much more difficult to allow others to carry the project. One of our colleagues who uses group work successfully in the traditional classroom has developed a unique way to encourage uniform group participation. He allocates a number of total points to each group assignment and requires the group to allocate the points among its members. If the assignment is done well and the points are allocated evenly, each member receives the number needed to maintain an A.

Peer Review

A simple and useful technique for student interaction is to ask them to review each others' work. Our experience is that this technique is most successful when students serve as reviewers at the draft stage, allowing peers to point out errors, suggest changes, and comment on topics and content without having to evaluate overall quality. We also suggest that each student have at least two reviewers—reducing the chances of receiving a single, weak review or of placing blame on the reviewer if recommendations are adopted and the assignment does not do as well as the author anticipated.

Brainstorming

A useful way to get students together through live chat or in a virtual classroom is to have them brainstorm a topic for later input into a larger discussion. For example, if you are planning to discuss a question on the class discussion board about what contribution the early inhabitants of the Indus River Valley had on the development of Hindu philosophy, you might begin by asking smaller groups to brainstorm the question. Here again, it is helpful to invite students to develop their initial ideas independently and bring these to their group. They can then synthesize what they consider to be their best thoughts and post them to the discussion board as a team. (This may appear to be an unnecessary combination of individual and group input, but one of the most significant challenges of group activity is encouraging even participation.)

Debates

Debates can be useful ways to encourage teams to work through ideas or issues before going onto the discussion board. However, debates work most suc-

cessfully as collaborative learning experiences when two or more members represent each position, research topics as a team, then debate with another team either synchronously or asynchronously. They can then provide a summary or synopsis to the teacher or class at large. Much of the collaborative value comes from jointly researching and refining the topic with a partner, while the summary to the class encourages each team to do its best and not simply brush off the assignment.

Online Resources

Instructor Tony Erben's home page: www.coedu.usf.edu/terben/FL/FL_links.htm

Free templates for creating games: www.netxv.net/esc/technology/Instructional Technology/templates/powerpoint.htm

Teaching Tip

Use chat rooms sparingly. Adult learners' schedules aren't conducive to requiring set online times. When using chat rooms, manage the discussion in small chunks of topics and times and provide discussion guidelines, and ask students to use each other's names when responding. Keep online groups small—no more than three per group. Assign students to groups and give them a preliminary "get to know you" assignment such as identifying the top 10 things that make groups successful or fail, and have them create group ground rules for completing tasks. Keep the same group together throughout the semester to reduce anxiety and let group members concentrate on getting to know each other and do the work they need to do together.

—Terri Langan
instructional development and delivery
Fox Valley Technical College, Wisconsin

> ### Teaching Tip
>
> Use groups to have students help each other with projects or essays. However, assign specific tasks to each person in the group to help them organize their group and time. In chat rooms, have a specific focus for the discussion, and facilitate that discussion by asking more questions.
>
> —Jaclyn Allen
> online English instructor
> Bismarck State College, North Dakota

Group Presentations and Panels

Using the discussion board, chat function, or virtual classroom, you can assign groups to make presentations or direct the class in dialogue about an assigned topic. Again, this can be either synchronous or asynchronous and can be a graded or less formal assignment. Some faculty choose to make every discussion a small group exercise first, requiring that assigned groups get together before the broader discussion to formulate their thoughts. The instructor can then feel more confident asking any one of the smaller groups to lead the rest in discussion, much as you might use a panel or team-led dialogue in a face-to-face setting.

Think–Pair–Share

A commonly used on-ground active learning technique is a Think–Pair–Share, which generally follows other study or discussion. This exercise invites students individually to spend time processing what they have learned, then to match up with one or more others to share their thoughts about the topic. It is less formal than most of the techniques previously mentioned, but it is an excellent way to process and reinforce newly gained knowledge.

Role Playing

You might think of role playing as limited to face-to-face interaction, but it can work equally well online. In

a history class, for example, a group of students might be assigned to be Civil War–era newspaper reporters, charged with conducting an interview with General Sherman following his march through the South. Your student who draws the Sherman role then must defend his actions to this 1860s press corps inquisition. In a business law or office management course, the exchange might be between an employer and employee, simulating an interview and focusing on the kinds of questions that may or may not be legal.

Paired Practice

One of the most creative and successful online teachers we know is Tony Erben, who teaches modern language at Florida South University. Erben's students use webcams and microphones to practice speaking to each other, with an expectation that they will log a specified amount of paired practice time each week. Tony teaches a number of languages online, including Japanese, and his homepage is a wonderful resource for practice exercises and collaborative tools. Tony maintains that his Web-instructed students perform as well as, or better than, his traditional classroom-based sections on both written and oral assessments.

Games

Erben's Web site also contains directions to a number of useful interactive games. Some talented online teachers

> ### Teaching Tip
>
> Online courses are ripe environments for collaboration. Require a percentage of collaborative activities where the content is conducive to collaborative learning. Use "teach-to-learn" activities that require small groups to take a chunk of content you assign to them and teach it to the rest of the class. Participate as a follow-up facilitator of discussion.
>
> —Terri Langan
> instructional development and delivery
> Fox Valley Technical College, Wisconsin

effectively use games as part of their active learning strategies. There are, for example, templates for the popular TV quiz game *Jeopardy* available on the Web that allow you to formulate your own categories and questions. Students can be paired or grouped in small teams to work their way though a *Jeopardy* game as a section review or in preparation for an exam.

We remind you again, however, that if you are new to online teaching, begin with the simple. Engage students in the more basic collaborative exercises first—in peer review, small group work, presentations, and the like and progress to more elaborate activities as you mature as an online teacher and as you learn more about how ably your students can use various technologies. But learn to use the group tools early. They can be some of your most useful instructional allies.

Teaching Tip

Place students in groups to review each other's projects and papers. Provide specific instructions to give feedback for their peers' work. Where applicable, have students role play when using interactive tools and simulations; for example, one student might be in charge of gathering data for another to run through a simulation, which another receives to process.

—Jaclyn Allen
online English instructor
Bismarck State College, North Dakota

CHAPTER 9

Bells and Whistles

In this chapter, we discuss some of the more sophisticated tools available to online instructors to enhance their materials and courses. We explain how to access, create, or develop some of these tools.

Most of us who teach online are not computer experts, but we do have a rudimentary grasp of the technology. We can all word process, create files, transfer textual information from one place to another, e-mail, and manage our class documentation effectively. We can even decorate our pages to some degree using color and font preferences, shading, and outlines—using the standard tools that come with the computer. But from that point, the technical savvy of community college online instructors differs appreciably from one to another.

Therefore, this chapter presumes some familiarity with the Web, but not much. The attempt here is to describe the fundamentals of various sight and sound options sufficiently to allow new online instructors enough information to incorporate at least some of them into their courses. However, avoid getting bogged down with window dressing to the point that you neglect what is most important for any online instructor: learning.

To date, many colleges still offer little in the way of course development training for new online teachers, particularly training that goes beyond the basics. But that situation is changing rapidly. Institutions across the United States are initiating programs to teach instructors not only basic course development but also how to use the extras available to them.

One example is the Illinois Online Network at the University of Illinois at Urbana, which has deployed e-learning with the help of a product called Elluminate to aid in incorporating real-time interaction to asynchronous courses. According to program director Michael W. Lindeman, the network is currently providing faculty development mostly to community college instructors.

Be forewarned that adding bells and whistles can get complicated for both you and your students. The more things you include (aside from simple graphics), the more the student will have to download or manipulate in some fashion, and that takes even more of their time. Choose your creative additions carefully—in this case, form should follow function. Conversely, a few well-selected choices can add considerable pizzazz and instructional impact to your course site through the use of just a few basics. We have included in this chapter a list of Internet resources that offer tutorials for each of the methods outlined.

Enhanced Graphics

Few people would disagree that we live in a visually oriented society. Those in the business of promoting

Bells and Whistles

fonts	music
style	sound bites
color	recorded lectures
background	video or film clips
clipart	HTML
animation	webcams
photos	

political agendas, candidates, information, facilities, services, events, or commercial ventures seek to draw attention to their products through the artful manipulation of sight, sound, and sensation. Even the evening news bombards us with special effects, live action, and reenactments of events that rival Hollywood films. In fact most Americans have grown up in an environment that has relentlessly solicited their visual and aural attention. So when your students log on to your class, do not be surprised if they expect something more than black 12-point Times New Roman font on a plain white page. This does not mean your online class should look like a highway billboard or a vacation brochure—in other words, less than academic. But embellishments that add to the efficiency of the instruction or better engage the student can be a good thing.

Effective graphic design creates visual logic and achieves a balance between visual sensation and actual information. Without the visual impact of shape, color, and contrast, pages are graphically uninteresting, and students may be less inclined to linger long enough to absorb the information. Or they may have difficulty prioritizing what is most important and what is supplemental information. As was mentioned earlier, structure is critical to many learners, especially those who are academically less mature.

Dense text documents without contrast and visual relief are also harder to read, especially on the relatively low-resolution screens of many personal computers. Without the depth and complexity of text, highly graphical pages risk the suggestion of marginalizing the academic content. Enhancing the

look of your course pages can be as simple as changing the font. You can make an ordinary document visually intriguing by doing nothing more than enlarging titles and topics, adding color, and manipulating font. Shading or outlining areas you want to draw your students' attention to can add dimension and visual interest as well. Just a few simple changes can make a page more attractive, add character, relate it more directly to your course, and bring attention to the areas you want students to notice first.

A good way to begin is to look at your textual information and imagine how you would ideally like for a student to see and absorb that material—and in what sequence. When your student first looks at a page of information, it should be readily apparent what the primary subject matter is and the level of importance of the subcategories that fall within it. An easy way to guide your students through the text in the right sequence is simply to work with the font and paragraph settings. You can enlarge and colorize the main subject heading, then use progressively smaller font sizes and more subtle colors for the various subheadings. Special sections can be easily outlined or shaded to point out information that may stand on its own or that you want the student to be able to locate at a glance. (Note the comparison of a plain and graphically touched up syllabus shown in Figures 9.1 and 9.2.)

Pictures that relate to your subject matter also can be added. Clipart is easy to use, offers almost

Teaching Tip

Don't just load text; use graphics where appropriate. There are several free clipart sites as well as sites with clipart available for purchase. I also recommend using colors in your text—not a lot, but enough to help the eye move across the page to make it interesting. Use darker colors, because they print better and are easier to read.

—*Therese Millis*
online physical therapy instructor
San Juan College, New Mexico

unlimited images you can copy and paste onto your site, and is available on most computers through myriad free sites on the Web.

As we mentioned in the chapter on course organization, some faculty produce PowerPoint presentations for their classes to supplement lectures or for demonstration. Most of these graphic enhancements can be used in that format, but avoid creating slides that are overly decorated. However, if you are only going to produce a page of text, why bother with PowerPoint?

Animation

Adding animation gets more complicated. Most Web animation requires special plug-ins for viewing. The exception is the animated GIF format, which is by far the most prevalent animation format on the Web, followed closely by Macromedia's Flash format. The animation option of the GIF format combines GIF images into a single file to create animation. It is something like flipping through a stack of cartoon drawings to simulate movement. You can set the animation to loop on the page or to play once, and you can designate the duration for each frame in the animation.

Most of the software for making animations uses cells or frames. Typically a cell is created as a drawing or by importing a photograph or other graphic. The cell is then copied, and a new one is created with a slight change or movement, and so on. When they are played in fast sequence, your images appear to move.

Animated GIFs have several drawbacks. GIF animations do not provide control by the user, so students have no easy way to stop a looping animation short of closing the browser window. They also lack the means to replay nonlooping animation. GIF animations also tend to be large files. Before you import any you should probably compress them. Programs such as Macromedia Fireworks and others can be used to do that—just remember the more files you have of this variety, the slower the program will load for students using dialup.

The final drawback is a concern that pertains to animations in general. Most animation is nothing more

> ### Teaching Tip
>
> I use threaded discussions extensively in my classes, but the first one is strictly for fun: introducing ourselves to each other and making connections through questions and answers. I also try to follow principles of good design in putting together the course, so the content is reinforced by the format and so that it's more interesting than straight gray text.
>
> —Jane Schreck
> online English instructor
> Bismarck State College, North Dakota

than a distraction. If you place animation alongside instructional content, it may do no more than disrupt your students' concentration. If you do choose to try animation, one way to minimize the potential distraction is to present it in a secondary window. This technique offers the student the option of shutting down the animation and viewing just the text.

There is a place for animation on the Web: Simple animation on a Web site's main home page can provide just the right amount of visual interest to invite users to explore your materials. There, the essential content is typically a menu of links, so the threat of distraction is less than it would be on an internal content page. Subtle animation such as a rollover may help guide the student to interact with elements that they might otherwise overlook. Animation also can be useful in illustrating concepts or procedures, such as steps in a process.

Photos

Adding photographs to your pages is by far the easiest way to introduce visuals to your course. It is a relatively easy process and has few of the drawbacks (e.g., time consumption, downloading difficulties) of more sophisticated visuals, such as video clips. In addition, photos can apply directly to the subject at hand and be interspersed throughout the text without interrupting the reading process.

Figure 9.1. Example of a syllabus page before graphic enhancement.

COURSE SYLLABUS
Art History & Appreciation 101

Jane Smith, EdD
123@server.com
Home Office Telephone: 123-555-1212

Course Number: Art 101
Credit Hours: 3
Course Prerequisite: None

Course Description:
This course presents an overview of major art periods from Prehistoric times through the Middle Ages. It is designed to promote an understanding and appreciation of the various manifestations of art, their origins, impact, and current relevance. This course partially fulfills humanities general education requirements.

Student Abilities:
This course will address the following student abilities as identified by XYZ Community College as being important for personal development:

Communication:
Communication is the process by which a thought or impression is effectively moved through its unique mode from one person or source to another. This class focuses on visual art (painting, sculpture, architecture) as a method used to transpose abstract ideas and concepts into a tangible reality. This form of communication tracks art from Prehistoric times through the Middle Ages.

Cultural Awareness:
Cultural awareness is the recognition of and the appreciation for the unique components (e.g., history, social structure, religious beliefs, art, traditions, rituals) that define the inhabitants and properties of a particular world region. This class explores how different cultures make sense of their reality and use the vehicle of art to respond to it. Art 101 traces how man has responded to his culture from Prehistoric times to the Middle Ages.

Figure 9.2. Example of a syllabus enhanced with simple fonts and graphics tools.

COURSE SYLLABUS
Art History & Appreciation 101

JANE SMITH, EdD

123@server.com

Home Office Telephone: 123-555-1212

Course Number: Art 101

Credit Hours: 3

Course Prerequisite: None

COURSE DESCRIPTION

This course presents an overview of major art periods from Prehistoric times through the Middle Ages. It is designed to promote an understanding and appreciation of the various manifestations of art, their origins, impact, and current relevance. This course partially fulfills humanities general education requirements.

STUDENT ABILITIES

This course will address the following student abilities as identified by XYZ Community College as being important for personal development:

Communication: Communication is the process by which a thought or impression is effectively moved through its unique mode from one person or source to another.

This class focuses on visual art (painting, sculpture, architecture) as a method used to transpose abstract ideas and concepts into a tangible reality. This form of communication tracks art from Prehistoric times through the Middle Ages.

Cultural Awareness: Cultural awareness is the recognition of and the appreciation for the unique components (e.g., history, social structure, religious beliefs, art, traditions, rituals) that define the inhabitants and properties of a particular world region.

This class explores how different cultures make sense of their reality and use the vehicle of art to respond to it. Art 101 traces how man has responded to his culture from Prehistoric times to the Middle Ages.

You can scan in existing photographs using a color scanner, use a digital camera to create the image, or copy (with permission if the work is legally protected) existing photographs from the Web. Two graphics formats widely used in Web documents are GIF and JPEG. Most programs for editing photos (e.g., Adobe Photoshop) support these formats.

Where photographs are concerned, the use of a good paint application, conversion to JPEG format, and possible resizing of the photo works wonders for the file sizes. Do not set the JPEG to more than 50% compression, because the quality of the photograph will be degraded. Paint Shop Pro, PhotoShop, and many other paint applications will help you shrink the size of your graphic files without compromising their color or integrity. Use your paint application and experiment with different compression rates and sizes. View the results with your Web browser until you have the smallest files that look the same as the original.

It is also important to know that most sites on the Internet are made in the 800 x 600 pixel video format and at least high-color 16 bit. Using a larger number of pixels for your photograph will require most users to scroll sideways to view the entire page. In addition, your display will appear to be off center. Make sure your display is set to 800 x 600 pixels and at least high-color 16 bit, or better, before you begin.

Teaching Tip

Use colors, if you have that option. Use graphics, cartoons (appropriate!!). Keep it user friendly. Put a title on it so they will know what the heck it is. Everybody gets tired of plain old print—let them see a graphic or other illustration to complement your issue and focus. Some students are very visual learners; this just may be the trick to help them.

—*Joe Ellefson*
online instructor, criminal justice
Bismarck State College, North Dakota

If your machine does not have the video ram to support high-color, be sure to select 256 colors when asked about color resolution.

Photographs can be used in any number of ways. Faculty teaching geography, religious studies, history, or literature can develop folders containing photos of people and places related to subject units—scanned from printed photos or loaded directly into class file folders from a digital camera. An online building design instructor attempting to describe the construction and application of support beams might include building-site photographs of workers actually going through each step of the process. Biology faculty could "walk" students through a dissection. The possibilities are limited only by your imagination.

Photographs also can be used for things other than instruction. Some online teachers ask students to submit headshots and organize them into a class directory so everyone can see each other. Other faculty post photographs of important areas of the college or of various activities and events to better include online students who do not have the opportunity to get to the physical campus. With the availability of digital cameras, it is a simple process to take photographs and save them to your computer for use with your online class. They may then be copied and pasted on to documents or linked to instructional pages.

Slide shows are another means of delivering multimedia presentations to your class. In a slide show, you can synchronize audio with still images. This is a great way to present lectures or describe sequential procedures. Still images compress much more efficiently than video, and because slide shows do not require smooth motion, the movie frame rate can be low. This means that you can devote more data to image quality and size.

Audio

Audio is an extremely efficient way to deliver information to your students. Imagine offering your class a lecture on the topic at hand, supplemented by an audio track of you speaking the words. It renders options for those who learn better by one method of

Teaching Tip

Add a small graphic on the announcement page that may be changed to reflect the topic currently being studied or what is happening in the course—testing, grading, and the like. Graphics in other modules are useful also if downloading the screen is not a problem. Many students still have low-bandwidth modems. Require that students move through the course together as a class. Abandon self-paced ideas.

—*Jo Ann Armstrong*
online psychology and sociology instructor
Patrick Henry Community College, Virginia

delivery or another and offers convenience to students who may be in a better position to listen than to read—such as the working mother with children at hand or someone who has vision difficulties.

Sound can be added to Web pages in a couple of basic formats:

- Uncompressed sound (or wave) files are digital representations of sound, like the tracks on an audio CD. This category includes Windows wave (.wav), Macintosh AIFF (.aif), and Sun audio (.au), which was the original Web sound format.
- MIDI (Musical Instrument Digital Interface) files contain no sound at all. Instead they are instructions to a music synthesizer (like the one in your computer's sound card) telling it which notes to play, which instrument sounds to use, and other effects.

MIDI files are much smaller and therefore take less time to download than larger .au and .wav files. MIDI files can contain only background (instrumental) music whereas both au. files and .wav can contain any type of sounds (e.g., vocal, background).

Streaming audio (the first, and perhaps still best version is RealAudio) relies on a player, usually a browser plug-in, that plays the sound as it is received—"streaming in" as it goes, rather than waiting for the entire file to download. This medium is most suitable for speech, which can be sent at a lower quality and still sound good.

Audio can be captured and optimized with relative ease, and it compresses well. When recording original audio, take steps to produce a quality product for your students. Low-frequency background noises, for example, such as lawn mowers, dishwashers, or loud air conditioning units, will be inseparable from your audio track and can muddle the sound. Remember, too, that the "downsampling" and compression needed to make your audio Web deliverable will emphasize any flaws in your recording.

Sites such as Instant Web Audio provide step-by-step instructions for adding all sorts of sound to your Web pages. You can add welcome messages for your students as they log on at the beginning of the year. Or perhaps send audio postcards to your students instead of a typical text announcement. Adobe Audition is a fun product that enables you to "paint" your course with sound: tones, pieces of songs, and voices or miscellaneous noises.

Video

Since *I Love Lucy* invaded the living rooms of America in the 1950s, we have been a society focused on video. Hollywood's expansion into the home video market, the advent of MTV and the music video industry, and the rapid expansion of personal computer use, have all added to our love of moving pictures. When the Web first emerged, video clips rarely were used, because to watch them, you had to download the entire video file before you could see anything, which can be several megabytes for even short segments. Downloading could literally take hours. Later as Web technology evolved, solutions emerged that allowed video to be streamed to you. This means that when you ask for video (click on a Web page link), you start to see the video information as soon as enough has been sent to show you a portion, and the rest continues to stream in as you watch the beginning parts.

screen or page layout. However, perhaps the most useful component for the online instructor is the incorporation of links to information. Using HTML, you can specify links to any document on any server that is part of the Internet. The resource list in this chapter includes a number of sites that provide step-by-step tutorials for using HTML. Most of these offer the novice a basic walk-through of the process, as well as links to other sites containing more advanced information.

Webcams

Cameras are everywhere. Whether we are shopping, picking our kids up at school, or walking through Times Square, "Big Brother" is watching. Cameras are constantly viewing and recording activities, places, and events throughout the world and, in many cases, can stream these pictures live to any computer equipped to receive video. Used in an instructional context, webcams can provide a powerful educational tool.

Sites like Earthcam.com provide an amazing array of possibilities. By going to this site and clicking on the webcam choice you have designated, students can witness a place, event, or activity related to your course in real time via a camera stationed at that location. A sociology class can observe daily life in the city of Opole, Poland, whereas a course in political science might view Ground Zero or watch a debate in Congress. There are also information-specific sites (e.g., Webcam Search) where students can observe diverse activities such as volcanoes erupting, people working in an office, or chickens laying eggs.

Another use of webcams involves live transmission of the students themselves via small, digitized cameras attached to their computers. This synchronous discussion technique is especially valuable in language classes, where pairs can practice dialogue and see facial movement during pronunciation practice.

As with any bells and whistles, before investing your time and that of your students in webcam technology, consider the benefit. Is the content significant and observable? Will the experience add valuable information to your course? If so, webcams can be fun and worth the effort.

Bells and Whistles Without Technology

Adding detail and interest to the content of your online class does not have to be limited to computer technology. There are many creative ways to add excitement to the learning process, limited only to your imagination and time:

- Plan a class excursion to a centrally located place of interest—perhaps one that relates to the course. An online art history class might meet at a local gallery. A building class could meet at a construction site. It would be unrealistic to expect that in all cases, the majority of students would be able to show up for such an activity, but for those who are able, the excursion would undoubtedly enrich the learning experience. It is also a demonstration of the instructor's willingness to go the extra mile for the students.

- Have your students send their photographs and post them to a page, accompanied by their names and brief bios so that everyone can visualize and learn about their classmates.

- Create a page for student announcements—sort of a message board. Some platforms refer to these as sidebars or water cooler discussion forums. This page is not a place for academic discussion but instead provides a venue for students to wish others a happy birthday or tell the class about their vacation, for example.

CHAPTER 10

Getting Acquainted With Platforms

In this chapter, we provide a brief overview of the most commonly used platforms and discuss the major differences between them. We review new open-source systems, such as Moodle and Sakai, and examine the compatibility between these and commercial platforms.

Throughout this book, we have referred regularly to course management systems and platforms, and we have used examples from the primary ones. Major developments are under way that will affect how these systems will look in the future and will find greatest acceptance.

Primary Platforms

In recent years, two platforms have emerged as the mainstays of the industry: Blackboard and WebCT. In late 2005, Blackboard claimed that its e-learning system was the most widely used among U.S. postsecondary institutions (see www.blackboard.com/company), and WebCT presented itself as the leading international provider of e-learning solutions (see www.webct.com). Although each originated independently, in October of 2005 Blackboard, Inc., announced it was acquiring WebCT, Inc., for $180 million, with the new company remaining under the Blackboard name. At the time, the combined company brought together more than 3,700 clients, approximately 800 employees, and 7 offices in the United States and abroad.

It is impossible to know what will eventually emerge as an integrated course management product from this giant merger. Both of the platforms offer similar services in their separate iterations. WebCT is seen by its advocates as providing greater flexibility in creating a more customized homepage menu, whereas Blackboard proponents believe that its architecture is not as template driven in the content areas, providing greater flexibility to load and move files internally. Each platform affords small niceties that the other lacks, but both have been equally capable and similar enough that users can move quite easily from one to the other, once familiar with either. The online journal, *Inside Higher Ed* (Lederman, 2006), announced in late 2006 that there is also significant movement in the industry toward what is referred to as Common Cartridge—a set of formatting standards that will allow digital information to be displayed similarly on any course management system that uses the cartridge. Blackboard is one of the design participants.

There are a number of alternatives, and several offer attractive features to their subscribers. Companies with a share of the full-service e-learning market include Campus Pipeline, Convene ac@deme, eCollege.com, and e-Education. Each of these providers offers tools and services that assist institutions in creating, editing, and managing online courses and programs.

Course Development Providers

There are also a host of course development products, sites, and tools; some are free and some are commercially available. Faculty teaching online will benefit from scanning one of the Web sites that list dozens of these providers and describes their products and services. The following examples might entice you to take the time to do so. In many cases, sites such as these will include links to other useful locations, and you can gradually build a catalog of the most useful Internet resources for your particular courses and interests.

- Hot Potatoes. This software tool is not free, but it is available at no cost to nonprofit educational organizations. Its applications include assistance with creating multiple choice and short answer tests, crosswords, and other learning exercises.
- MIT's OpenCourseWare. MIT provides access to a full catalog of free course materials for educators in the nonprofit sector, students, and learners.
- Purdue University Online Writing Lab. This comprehensive and user-friendly site offers assistance with student questions concerning writing, research, and style formats.
- Active Reviewing Guide. Originating in the United Kingdom, this site offers excellent tips for reviewing material through questioning techniques, group review, and so forth.
- Parade of Games in PowerPoint. Trivia, Jeopardy, and Scavenger Hunt are a few of the templates for creating learning games provided by this site, in addition to a link to the author's favorite game sites.

Open-Source Course Management Systems

Perhaps the most significant development in course management systems in recent years has been the creation of open-source or free platforms. These systems are the creations of technology specialists who believe that e-learning solutions should be

available to anyone, without cost. Perhaps the two most prominent open-source learning systems are Moodle and Sakai.

Sakai

The Sakai Project began in 2004 when four major universities—University of Michigan–Ann Arbor, Indiana University, Massachusetts Institute of Technology, and Stanford University—pooled their work on course management development and, with the assistance of the Mellon Foundation, formed Sakai (see www.collab.sakaiproject.org/portal). The goals of the project are to create a course management system that contains and improves on the best features of existing systems, provides an accompanying research component, and is available to learning institutions at no cost.

The list of those experimenting with Sakai includes many of the top universities in the United States: University of California at Berkeley, Columbia University, Johns Hopkins University, Northwestern University, Rice University, and Yale University, to name a few. California's Foothill-De Anza Community College District piloted a project in 2005 with 30 other California community colleges to evaluate whether the platform might serve their distance learning needs in the future. Foothill-De Anza is using Sakai for a program called Sofia that places free courseware on the Web for use by any interested educator (http://sofia.fhda.edu/overview.htm#Evaluation). Sakai will be playing a major role in platform development over the next several decades and, as mentioned earlier, is a contributor to the Common Cartridge development work (Lederman, 2006).

Moodle

Moodle has a much less elegant, but more interesting, origin (see http://moodle.org). It was the brainchild of Martin Dougiamas, who served during the 1990s as webmaster for Curtin University of

Technology. He became disenchanted with what he viewed as the cumbersome nature of the major commercial online learning platforms and resolved to create his own. Moodle differs from Sakai in that it has completely open architecture, and, although Dougiamas continues to serve as project leader, the system is shaped and developed by its users. It relies philosophically on the concepts of social constructionist pedagogy that we referred to in chapter 7—

Resources for Course Management Platforms

Course Management Platforms

Blackboard	http://blackboard.com
WebCT	www.webct.com
Campus Pipeline	www.sct.com/Education/products/p_cl_campuspipeline.html
Convene	www.convene.com
eCollege	www.ecollege.com/indexflash.learn
e-Education	www.eeducation.com.au

Course Development Tools and Guides

Active Reviewing Guide	www.reviewing.co.uk
Hot Potatoes	http://web.uvic.ca/hrd/hotpot
Integrating the Internet Into the Classroom	www.lclark.edu/krauss/usia/home.html
Let's Create Web-based Learning Activities	www.lclark.edu/~krauss/ORTESOL2000web/home.html#
List of tools and guides	www.web-miner.com/detools.htm
MIT's OpenCourseWare	http://ocw.mit.edu/index.html
Parade of Games in PowerPoint	http://facstaff.uww.edu/jonesd/games
Purdue University Online Writing Lab	http://owl.english.purdue.edu
Quia	www.quia.com/web
Teaching & Learning on the Web	www.mcli.dist.maricopa.edu/tl/index.html

Open-Source Course Management Systems

Moodle	http://moodle.com
moodlerooms	http://facultyroom.org
Sakai	www.sakaiproject.org

Note. This list of Web sites includes our best current suggestions for finding additional information related to this chapter. However, because the Internet is continually changing, we suggest that if sites have become inactive, or further information is desired, the reader enter one of the following descriptors into a Web search tool and see what is current: E-learning, course development, course management systems, or open-source course management systems.

the idea that learning and knowledge are extensions of the environment in which the learning occurs.

Essentially, Moodle users contribute ideas, modules, learning activities, and so forth. Contributors agree to honor the copyright, but may use it, modify it, and contribute to new releases as long as they work within the terms of the licensing agreement. The Moodle platform has been evolving since 1999 and has been translated into 61 languages. As of this writing, more than 3,300 sites from 114 countries are registered with Moodle, and its programs are being downloaded more than 500 times a day.

Moodle presents most of the features of the major e-learning platforms, and, because it is open source, it is developing rapidly. One of its most attractive features is that it is topic oriented, rather than being function oriented as are most e-learning platforms. This means that everything is organized around sections (topics), which have their own tools (such as forums and quizzes), whereas most e-learning platforms are organized around tools such as course information, communication, and the like. Moodle's main strength (and perhaps also its main weakness) is that it is in a constant state of evolution as its 7,000 contributors worldwide work to modify and improve it.

Karen Klos, a colleague who serves as online course manager for East Central Community College, has begun the process of introducing Moodle as an alternative for faculty at her institution. Her hope is that eventually East Central may be able to transition entirely to this open-source provider. As of this writing, she reported that there are still a number of transitional bugs to work out, but with each new release, the platform becomes more stable and bug free.

How do faculty like it? Some prefer Moodle because it is so easy to navigate—much more instinctual than other programs. You can turn on an edit mode on the home page and work on modifications without having to navigate to a particular section. Other faculty members find the occasional bugs too unnerving to be willing to trust a fast-moving and schedule-driven class to it at this point. It appears that those who are most comfortable with technology

Teaching Tip

No matter how good a college's technical support may be, it's the online instructor who must be prepared to deal with technical glitches as they arise and to help students with the technical problems they encounter. The instructor must know as much as possible about all technology used in the course—from the course management system, to e-mail, to any software programs required for the class.

—Jim Burns
online English instructor
Mountain Empire Community College,
Virginia

find Moodle fun, fast, flexible, and enticing, whereas the less familiar prefer the comfort of the established systems and protocols. Karen reported

Although the free aspect of the software is great, there has been some significant time invested this semester. We'll have to see how the new versions run and are still weighing the pros and cons of making it a mandatory campus-wide tool. We're also waiting like everyone else to see what the Blackboard/WebCT merge will bring forth (financially and creatively). (K. Klos, personal communication, December 19, 2005)

Karen's comments are a reasonable summation of the current state of course management system development. Open-source systems will undoubtedly find a place in the market—perhaps a significant one as they perfect their platforms and services. Commercial providers will undoubtedly continue to consolidate. Their abilities to compete will probably depend on how capably they can maintain an innovative edge and how completely they cover the array of support services that are difficult for open-source providers to provide and maintain.

CHAPTER 11

In Loco Parentis Online

In this chapter, we suggest that online instructors should, in spite of physical distance and some degree of anonymity, interact with their students in a personal and caring way. An online classroom can be a surprisingly warm and welcoming place with a hands-on instructor who serves as leader, mentor, facilitator, and student advocate. We describe techniques for interjecting a sense of interest and enthusiasm into the course that aids students' performance and retention.

In higher education, quality of learning is measured in many ways. Quality includes access to good learning resources and facilities such as libraries and laboratories. But it also should include effective development via student-to-student interaction and meaningful personal contact with instructors. It implies well-developed course content, diverse and applicable student experiences, and uniform rigor in expectation. The latter issues are areas in which distance learning has been vulnerable to criticism. Some critics believe our academic traditions, especially the important component of student inclusion in the campus culture, are being threatened by the expansion of distance learning. Could the familial bond between professor and student, which was part and parcel of the first academic communities set up, eventually die out with the depersonalization of computer-generated degrees? If we agree that this may be the direction education is heading and that personal interaction is important for students, then we must find ways to create those connections in the online environment.

The doctrine of in loco parentis was imported from English law as protection for teachers who felt the need to administer corporal punishment to students. William Blackstone may have been the first to apply the phrase in loco parentis to educators in his 1770 compilation of English law. By definition, teachers were given the right to act as parents when responding to disciplinary problems. Courts have been cautious in its administration, however, in light of contextual considerations such as the nature of the infraction, the method of discipline, and the age of the student (Conte, 2000). But over time, the term has come to imply more than legal protection. It refers to the idea that it is sometimes appropriate for educators to act in a parental capacity on their students' behalf, helping guide them toward academic success through a combination of teaching, personal attention, and genuine caring.

Contrary to rumors, the in loco parentis doctrine is alive and well in higher education, and colleges still exercise paternalistic control over most aspects of academic policy and many other phases of student life. A big part of the assumed responsibility of faculty and administrators alike is to help make students feel involved and included in the educational process, as well as with the institution itself and the people in it. This interpretation is particularly consistent with the community college philosophy that stresses personal care and concern.

Many educators suggest that a prudent adherence to in loco parentis ideals is essential to promote students' satisfaction and academic success. Research findings, such as those of Tinto in his highly touted *Theory of Departure* and of many others, support this prudent approach (Pascarella & Terenzini, 1991). Tinto's research revealed that the majority of students decide during the first few weeks of freshman year whether or not to remain at the institution. And further studies, such as McClelland's *Theory of Student Involvement,* demonstrate that "feeling involved and a part of the campus community" is the single most important factor in that decision (cited in Pascarella & Terenzini, 1991).

Colleges interested in retention and student success must foster an environment where students feel connected to the learning process, the institution, and the people—the involvement needs to start the minute students enroll. Although campus activities, student organizations, and orientations can be wonderful agents for involving students, personal interaction with caring faculty has been shown to be one of the strongest catalysts for connecting students to the university. When asked what made their college stay rewarding and why they chose to remain at their institution, students often have attributed at least some portion of their satisfaction to positive interaction with various teachers—more specifically, a feeling that their instructors took a personal interest in them and their academic success. That is, they cared (Pascarella & Terenzini, 1991).

If creating and retaining happy, satisfied students who do not drop out of our classes (or institutions) requires student involvement spawned by personal interaction, are online instructors at a huge disadvantage? Not at all. Even though the perceived loss of personal contact has always been one of the central criticisms espoused by distance education's detractors, in fact, online faculty have many means at their disposal for meaningful and personal interaction with students.

From the Instructor's Perspective

Most faculty are trained in "hand-to-hand" teaching. They expect and are accustomed to direct engagement with the students. The 2000 *American Faculty Poll* confirmed this in its finding that one of the most important factors for faculty in their decision to pursue an academic career was the enjoyment of working with students (Sanderson, Phua, & Herda, 2000).

In the traditional classroom, a skilled instructor will use her or his understanding of the audience to monitor reactions through observation of body language, verbal response, and eye contact, thereby creating an effective and multifaceted learning experience. Feedback is immediate and rich in information. For some online instructors, the lack of direct personal contact with students is a big issue and one of the chief reasons many resist moving into the area of Web education.

Faculty who teach online have little face-to-face contact or feedback to help them gauge the clarity of their communications. Students' responses in distance learning are often delayed and indirect. Rarely will there be the opportunity for hand-to-hand interaction with students learning at distant sites. The presumption is that the technology interface of distance learning often denies faculty this opportu-

---

Figure 11.1. Example of a Quick Reference Chart

SPRING 2007	ART HISTORY 101 ONLINE
Contact	Biography
Adam Akins AKT@AOL.COM 555-555-1212	18 Baseball scholarship Born and raised locally First semester in college First generation in college Taking this course because it's required Doesn't like art classes Family farms turkeys Active in 4H Enjoys country music and action movies Sister getting ready to have a baby

Bonnie Belvecio
BBEL@ZNET.COM
555-555-1213
	24
	Three small children
	Never married
	Italian family
	Loves to sketch and cook
	Draws unemployment
	Dropped out of high school then got GED and
	    is trying to complete a nursing degree
	Says she's fearful of being able to do the
	    college work

Charles Chan CHAN@EART.COM 555-555-1214	38 Firefighter for 15 years—now volunteers Loves reading Sorry he missed college and wants to start with CC then get a BA in history Married with two teenagers Daughter has serious medical condition

---

nity entirely. In fact, there are ways to avert much of the potential isolation that looms before both instructor and student in the online environment.

Online learning demands new skills for both the instructor and the student. As we stressed in the previous chapters, Web-based instruction shifts the educational experience from a teacher-centered atmosphere to a more learner-centered atmosphere.

Instructors serve primarily as facilitators or intermediaries between the students and the resources they need for their own collaborative or independent study. Nevertheless, within that capacity, instructors can create a climate of inclusion, involvement, and personal interest. In short, online faculty can exercise a degree of in loco parentis behavior in spite of the lack of face-to-face interaction.

Teaching Tips

Fostering Responsibility for Meeting Deadlines

Online instructors should expect technology glitches to be used by students on occasion as an excuse—legitimate or not—for missing deadlines. The following tips address this issue in constructive ways.

Life and technology issues can interrupt a student's ability to complete an assignment. I allow each student to turn in one assignment late during the semester. This allows them to complete the course outcomes and reduces my stress in trying to decide whether the excuse is significant enough to allow the late assignment.

—*Elizabeth Luzar*
online nursing instructor
Butler Community College, Kansas

Recognizing that technology will undoubtedly fail at least once during the semester, I give students one "technology pass" each per semester. They can use it to turn in one assignment late if they experience a technology glitch. If a student still has the unused pass at the end of the semester, he or she can use it for a few extra-credit points.

—*Chris Rubio*
online English instructor
American River College, California

I make assignments and tests due during times when students are more likely to have Internet access in places such as libraries. This helps eliminate excuses for lateness such as "my computer crashed this weekend, and I could not find any place to access the Internet and turn in my assignment."

—*Elizabeth Luzar*
online nursing instructor
Butler Community College, Kansas

Provide an FAQs page about learning and working online. Include directions like these to let students know how to communicate difficulties: "We all get sick. Computers hiccup. Storms take power lines down. Tragedies and celebrations happen. If these or other things occur, be sure to call me and let me know what's going on. If you are in the middle of a team project, be sure to call at least one of your team members and pass on the word. We'll discuss the situation and see what adjustments can be made."

—*Terri Langan*
instructional development and delivery
Fox Valley Technical College, Wisconsin

Remember that not all of your students have broadband Internet access; some of them may be using 14.4K dial-up for your class. If you are incorporating a lot of multimedia material in your assignments or assessments, download time can be a significant issue. LView Pro (www.lview.com) does a wonderful job of compressing large image files. It may be appropriate to mail your instructional materials to students on CDs rather than having them download the materials.

A student may claim that an assignment was submitted in a timely manner, but that it was lost or delayed during transmission to the server (that could be true). Tell the student to send you an electronic file copy of the assignment; that way, you can check the time and date of creation of a MS Word document by examining its properties (File/Properties/Statistics).

—*Herb Schade*
online physical science instructor
Crowder College, Missouri

The following sections suggest some ways to interact with online students, get to know who they are as unique people, and make them feel not just a part of a class led by a caring instructor but a part of an institution that has their best interests at heart.

First and Foremost, Know Who Your Students Are

The single most important way to begin building personal connections with your students is simply to take the time to know who they are. If you do that, you will already be ahead of the game and a step ahead of many instructors in traditional classrooms.

In addition to requesting and documenting brief biographical sketches of students as described in chapter 3, some instructors suggest that everyone send photographs to post alongside their information. Remember to post your own photograph and bio too. If your students are scattered around the state, or perhaps several states or countries, post a map and mark it to show where everyone is.

Another way to start the personal connection process is to make informal class introductions the subject of your first discussion forum or discussion board, as recommended in chapter 3. As an alternative or in addition to the posted bios, everyone can submit "bio threads" to initiate class chatter and initial interaction. It is wise to remind the students that this first discussion is casual but that the weekly course discussions to follow are to be related to the subject matter at hand and devoid of personal greeting or commentary.

It is also useful to create a chart for yourself and keep it handy (see Figure 11.1). List each student's name with a condensed version of his or her bio and contact information next to it. It serves as a great quick reference. Refer to it when you have cause to contact students individually to remind you of whom you are addressing. Are you e-mailing a 40-year-old retired military officer with college-aged kids, an 18-year-old freshman baseball player from a wealthy local family, a single mother of three who is holding down two jobs and taking courses at night? This information can make a decided difference in both expectation and approach.

Including something as simple in your communication as "I hope your daughter is doing well" can be surprisingly meaningful for online students who often enroll in distance education courses expecting an isolated and anonymous experience. The idea that the instructor actually knows who they are and takes the time to make a personal inquiry beyond the scope of academics can be enormously encouraging. Creating an atmosphere of personal interaction with your online students accomplishes more than getting them involved and providing a caring environment. By taking the time to know who the students are in real life, you will be able to better assess both their potential and their progress and guide their learning experience more efficiently.

Meeting Your Students in Person

It is not necessary to meet your online students to successfully interact with them on a personal basis. Sometimes a genuine online effort is all a dynamic instructor needs to connect with his or her students. However, some of the best distance-delivered courses have well-integrated components in which teachers do meet directly with students—individually, in small groups, or with the entire class.

If personal interaction between the teacher and students is deemed to be an important course component, it is critical to meet as a group as early in the semester as possible. Experienced distance education faculty report that students' comfort levels increase significantly if the students and instructor meet early in the course and develop a personal working relationship. Instructors also have reported that when students meet face-to-face late in the semester, the impressions about class members that have evolved online may be

---

How to Make Personal Connections With Your Online Students

- Before the semester begins, send each student a welcome letter via U.S. mail.

- Know who your students are by collecting, sharing, and referring to bios.

- Post a locator map so the class can get a sense of where everyone is.

- Construct a message board for student comments and informal exchange.

- Post announcements about upcoming activities on the physical campus and encourage your online students to participate.

- Take and post photographs of campus activities for your class.

- Find out everyone's birthdays and acknowledge them.

- Always remember your class on holidays, and post an appropriate greeting.

- Some time midsemester, send each student a personal note with a progress update.

- When appropriate, share personal information about yourself with the class.

- If you have the chance to include a class gathering or field trip of some sort, make it a point to have a conversation with every student in attendance. Make name tags. Have refreshments, if possible, and promote the social component too. Take photographs of the session and post them on the message board.

---

either reinforced or dashed, with mixed consequences. Therefore, if you are going to try to get your class together, it is probably a good idea to do it early.

Depending on proximity in your particular situation, it may or may not be possible, or even practical, to bring the class together in some physical location. Nevertheless, it is better to rule out personal contact as impractical or instructionally irrelevant than to fail to consider it in the first place. When the logistics can be successfully navigated, teachers and students alike are rewarded by well-planned and interactive face-to-face contact. Students report that participation in weekly or biweekly synchronous discussion provides some of the same value as face-to-face meetings and helps them feel connected. This may be considered as an alternative if actual meetings cannot be arranged because of time or distance constraints.

Aside from meeting in person, student-to-student interaction can be promoted through manipulation of study groups. Forming small groups for learning purposes (two to four students) often results in some level of personal interaction among the people. If you use the opportunity to spend time with each of the small groups as they work on their assigned tasks, teacher–student interaction is enriched.

Online students can have a satisfying learning experience, complete with personal interaction and a sense of involvement. Nevertheless, as with any teaching situation, it is up to the instructor to make this happen. A commitment to student advocacy, a determination to connect on a personal level with each student, and a healthy dose of in loco parentis can change your online class from a potentially isolated experience to one of inclusion.

Fostering Responsible Students

As with biological parents, educators who embrace an in loco parentis attitude seek to guide and advise their charges, while at the same time teaching them how to be responsible and independent so that they can leave the nest and fly alone. Students share responsibility with their instructors in the acquisition of a good learning experience, and some need more help than others in figuring out just what those responsibilities are and how to carry them out.

Therefore, another important component of your interaction with online students is to help them understand the critical importance of class participation, timely discussion responses, adherence to project deadlines, and learning to be a self-starter. Students also must be ethical in their procurement and dissemination of resource materials and honest about the originality of their submitted assignments. You may find that you have students who are fresh out of high school, enrolled in their first community college class, who need your extra attention to both understand their responsibilities and put them into practice. Some may need to be reminded about their ethical responsibilities. Copying someone else's work, as pointed out elsewhere in this book, is often a temptation for those less acclimated to the college environment.

This is an area where the online teacher has a decided edge. We all remember the student in high school who always sat in the back of the class, never raised his or her hand, and routinely made poor grades. Such students become amazingly astute at being invisible. The teachers know who they are. Unfortunately, overfull classes and cramped schedules often make it impossible for teachers to give these students the help they need to catch up.

One of the wonderful things about online learning in a community college, from a pedagogical standpoint, is that it often presents new and shining opportunities for those students who need extra guidance, and the format presents new ways for you to offer help. Simply put, online students lose their ability to hide in the back of the class. It is immediately apparent when they do not respond. As soon as you identify who they are, sometimes a few personal e-mails can make an enormous and immediate difference in the student's level of participation, not to mention his or her feeling of connection with faculty. For some, who have successfully avoided such contact for so long, it can be nothing short of a revelation.

One of us (Farnsworth) recalls sending a complimentary note about writing ability to the wrong student by mistake. I had intended it for a student who showed remarkable talent as a writer, telling her how much I appreciated the thought and effort she put into her work. It was early in the semester, and, without checking the names carefully, I addressed the compliment to another student. Fortunately, the other student was a decent writer also. She thanked me for the note, and the remarkable thing was that her writing immediately became much better. She wrote to my level of expectation, so to speak. We may often be inclined to ask too little of students—particularly those who have been academic wallflowers in the past. Online instruction provides an opportunity to single them out in positive and helpful ways.

In summary, the concept of in loco parentis takes on a whole new meaning for community college online instructors. It allows us to connect in a direct and surprisingly personal way with our students, offering a brand new avenue of opportunities not only to help promote those who are already academically able but also to reach down and pull up others who have fallen through the cracks.

CHAPTER 12

Encouraging Independent Work and Addressing Academic Dishonesty

Detecting and preventing online cheating, including plagiarism, and encouraging independent work from students are topics in this chapter. We discuss ways to ensure that students are doing their own work, techniques for assessing students in online classes, and ways to use assessment as an additional learning tool. A hypothetical example of academic dishonesty is provided, along with examples of how the problem was addressed and resolved.

Online cheating, or academic dishonesty, is identified by faculty as one of the most challenging issues they have to deal with. Jane Schreck of Bismarck State College observed,

I think this is a big problem online, partly because it's harder to monitor than in on-ground classes and partly because students seem more willing to cheat with an instructor they have never met. In the worst plagiarism I ever had, five students, all older-than-average women, turned in text from Web sites for an assignment on "writing effective instructions." I changed that assignment after that. I think we have some responsibility to avoid tempting students with cheating, but I suppose someone determined to cheat will be hard to stop. (J. Schreck, personal communication, December 19, 2005)

Strategies for Detecting and Preventing Academic Dishonesty

Students copying material directly from other sources without attribution reportedly is a major problem. Many have an amazing ability to find, copy, and paste Internet materials of all varieties, often word for word. As experienced English instructors know, there are a number of telltale signs. Are there sudden changes in sentence structure, style, and vocabulary? If printed, are there changes in font or other formatting elements in the submitted assignment? Does the work as a whole reflect what the teacher has seen in other submitted work in quality and style? It should, of course, be a standard expectation that all referenced work will be cited, allowing you to check where students say they found their material. By looking at these references, you may find that much of the rest of what appears to be stylistically different material came from the same source.

The Internet has done two things for plagiarism—given students access to an almost limitless library of written material about virtually any subject and given instructors electronic tools to find that same material. One of the best tools for detecting plagiarism is Google, which can locate a snippet of text if entered into its search box. There are also a number of excellent plagiarism search programs that are linked to major online research paper catalogs and other sources of electronically available information.

An important first, however, is to clearly spell out your policies and those of the institution in your syllabus and draw students' attention to these guidelines. Let them know before it becomes an issue that you routinely run a few phrases through a search engine and that there are effective ways to find borrowed material. As long as students are asked to write papers outside of a classroom setting, you will not be able to prevent them from getting help with written work. Your best measure of whether they are doing their own writing will be consistency. If you suspect that a student is not doing his or her own work, you may want to use some of the strategies outlined in this chapter.

Strategies for Encouraging Individual Work

The following are three strategies for ensuring that students do their own work.

- Create two (or more) written assignments and divide your class into sections, purposely separating students you know to be working together. Although many friends, roommates, or girlfriends might be willing to let someone copy or modify their work, most stop short of completing an entire assignment for another student.
- If there is a reading assignment, have students submit written responses to specific questions based on the reading. The questions can be phrased so that it is difficult for students to just paraphrase a section of the text, and at least students have the learning experience of writing down the information.
- Ask each student to come up with three pertinent questions relating to the subject being studied and to post their questions to the discussion board where everyone can add to the list. Indicate that no question can be duplicated. Everyone must read over the ones posted and come up with original questions. The assignment can then be to have each student respond to an assigned set of questions from the list.

Test Proctoring Strategies

Many of the same challenges that affect assessment of writing assignments apply to other forms of testing. If a student is taking a test using one of the course management systems' testing tools, how do you know who is actually filling in the responses? Unless you use proctors, you probably will not be sure. There are,

Teaching Tip

Design and enforce a uniform policy on academic integrity. Being strict from the beginning prevents problems later. Also, announce at the beginning of the course the requirement of a proctoring resource for at least two significant activities.

—*Jo Ann Armstrong*
online sociology and psychology instructor
Patrick Henry Community College, Virginia

however, ways to structure your use of tests and quizzes that minimize cheating.

Virtually all of the online testing tools have timing controls, allowing you to create your test, open it for student access at a specific time, and limit the amount of time students can work on the quiz or exam. You can notify students, for example, that the unit exam will be open at 8:00 a.m. Friday and will remain available until midnight of that night. Students will have an hour, once they open the test, to complete it. Once the test is finished and returned, students can no longer access it. You can time your tests by completing them yourself and see how much time it should take to complete the exam if you know the material well. Allow enough extra time for slower responders but not enough to look up each of the answers.

Some online teachers choose to make the testing instrument available only for the period of time needed to complete it—from 8:00 p.m. to 9:00 p.m. Thursday evening, for example—to prevent students from passing test information to others who take it later in the day. To accommodate students who may not have that hour available, they develop a morning version that is available from 7:00 a.m. to 8:00 a.m. the same day, but with a different set of questions. Quizzes can be handled similarly, with short time limits and several sets of questions.

If using multiple-choice assessments, most of the testing tools allow teachers to construct tests from a question pool that can create an exam for each student, selecting randomly from the questions assigned

to that pool. With this technique, every student is given a uniquely assembled test, and the tool corrects and scores each. The drawback with this approach is that unless you conduct an item analysis that monitors question difficulty, students can legitimately complain that they are not being equitably assessed. If you are willing to commit the time, this drawback can be overcome. Elizabeth Luzar, who teaches nursing at Butler Community College in Kansas, noted,

> I use question sets for online testing (the computer randomly selects a question from a pool of questions about a particular concept). This means that no student gets exactly the same test. I use item analysis data to maintain similar difficulty of the questions. (E. Luzar, personal communication, December 8, 2005)

Item analysis allows you or the computer program to determine, over time, which questions are missed with what frequency, establishing a rank ordering of difficulty that can be used for categorizing and sorting selections as tests are assembled.

No matter how you manage the testing, there will be cheating unless you arrange for a proctoring system. Some faculty use a proctor form that students must have completed and returned by the end of the second or third week of class. This form must be filled out with appropriate contact information by a responsible person who agrees to proctor exams for the students. Suitable proctors might include librarians, testing center personnel at a nearby college or high school, or a retired teacher who lives near the student. The instructor may, if there is any question, call the proctor and confirm legitimacy and suitability.

Tailoring Assessment for Online Students

Many of the online teaching experts we contacted while writing this handbook suggested that online student assessment, like development of online classes in general, invites new ways of thinking. As Terri Langan of Fox Valley Technical College in Wisconsin suggested, "Faculty and students should view assessment as opportunities to show off and

> ### Teaching Tip
>
> Give clear, focused directions for every assignment or discussion requirement. Respond to students often and constructively. Use students' names and encourage them to keep working. Provide summary status reports or reminders that they need to check their grades and status every 4 weeks or so in a semester-long course.
>
> —*Terri Langan*
> *instructional development and delivery*
> *Fox Valley Technical College, Wisconsin*

celebrate what has been learned. Assessment needs to be performance based" (T. Langan, personal communication, November 28, 2005). She reminds us of one of our colleagues who refers to her exams as "celebrations of learning."

You may wish to address the academic honesty issue in online classes by getting away from traditional testing approaches altogether. Find other evaluative means—presentations, directed discussion, or collaborative exercises—to evaluate what students have learned and how well they can apply the knowledge. If nothing else, you might rely on open-book written assessments that require students to synthesize knowledge in a way that forces them to bring together information from a number of sources. Finding someone to do this for them will be difficult enough that most will have to do the work themselves.

Returning to our world religions course example, you might ask students at the end of sections to respond in writing to questions such as the following:

Compare and contrast the views that Taoism, Confucianism, and Shinto have of the nature of the universe and our relationship to it. Describe how that relationship suggests how people should live and what is appropriate or moral conduct. Provide specific examples of how the world view of each translates into behavior, making China and Japan distinctive cultures.

Using Zoroastrianism and Judaism as your examples, develop a set of hypotheses or explanations about how religions develop and evolve. Why might Zoroastrianism differ from Hinduism so dramatically when they come from a common root? How might Zoroastrianism have affected Judaism's development? What do these explanations tell us about the evolution of religion in general? Use necessary facts, not just supposition, to support your conclusions and work toward at least two double-spaced pages of answers.

Assessment techniques of this variety bring us back to one of our pervasive themes: controlling time. And we repeat here that for this reason, class sizes in online courses should be determined using the standard that is applied to other time-intensive courses such as English composition.

Every instructor, whether online or on-ground, experiences roadblocks to good student assessment. Dealing with these in an online learning environment may actually improve your skills

> ### Teaching Tip
>
> Caring about students' progress and communicating with students to provide them with feedback and encouragement is vital. In addition, provide a personal touch to your course by communicating with students through e-mail, chats, and in announcements that keep students on track and inspires more interpersonal communication. Keeping the course organized and running smoothly can be accomplished by giving clear, concise, and unambiguous instructions.
>
> —*Jaclyn Allen*
> *online English instructor*
> *Bismarck State College, North Dakota*

as an evaluator of learning and may turn your evaluations into better learning experiences for your students. Each situation will differ, but common sense, a focus on professional and ethical behavior, and adherence to college policy and sound learning practice can do a great deal to improve the effectiveness of your teaching.

In the remainder of the chapter, we provide an example of a fictional instructor identifying and dealing with an instance of academic dishonesty. The example is a composite of information provided by a cross-section of online instructors.

Instructor Millie King Suspects Academic Dishonesty

It is late Sunday evening, and Millie has escaped to her upstairs home office to check in with her new online class. After graduate school, she taught for a few years at the state university, but her two young children were growing fast and needed more and more attention. Millie decided to spend a few years enjoying full-time mom status. She plans to return to full-time teaching down the road, but she is anxious to keep her skills fresh and stay in touch with the academic community. So, she agreed to teach an online class from home for a local community college that is expanding its distance education program. She can now be with her son and daughter and

still have time to devote to the field she loves.

So far the experience has been positive—a little different from conventional teaching to be sure, but the basics are the same. "If I suddenly lost my sight," Millie rationalized, "would I not still have the ability to teach?" She felt sure she would. "Then why shouldn't I be able to teach just as effectively online as I do in my classroom? My students are there. I just can't see them."

She has approached the opportunity primarily as being a matter of getting used to the technology and of figuring out the mechanics of the process. The college offered some orientation—frankly not that much. It is a small college and can fund only the most basic faculty development programs, but she has things up and running. This is her first experience with online teaching, so in many ways she is learning the online environment right along with her students.

It is exactly 1 week since Millie posted the first written assignment: a brief paper responding to a series of discussion questions about the first chapter on Paleolithic and Neolithic art. She labored over the questions, wanting to make her first assignment both fun and a great learning experience. Now she is eager to see how her new online students have responded.

Teaching Tip

Designing diverse activities and assignments, such as individual and group projects, discussions, essays, and so forth, helps instructors learn students' styles in their work. Knowing a student's style can help instructors identify possible cheating.

—*Jaclyn Allen*
online English instructor
Bismarck State College, North Dakota

With both children tucked into bed, Millie sits down at her computer with a cup of decaf tea and logs in. She signs onto Blackboard—the online teaching platform used by the community college—and a screen appears: "Welcome Millie!" She clicks on her course, then Control Panel, then Assignments.

And there they are! A long string of submitted assignments—several with salutatory headers: "This is my first paper Ms. King, please let me know if you don't get it"; or "Have a nice day!" Millie smiles. It looks like everyone has the work in on time! A couple at the last minute, one a few minutes late (10:00 p.m. was the established deadline) but not late enough to matter, she decides.

She begins downloading and reading assignments. The first paper is pretty good! Aside from being off a few millennia with the timeline (she makes a quick note to add that to her feedback), there are some thoughtful discussion responses. It's worth an *A*. The next several papers look good too. Millie is pleased with herself. Her students are clearly learning and are putting a lot of time into their responses.

As she begins reading the 10th paper, Millie notices something unusual. Hasn't she seen this misspelling before? What a coincidence that two students would mistake "hunters and gatherers" for "hunters and gardeners?" She looks back at the third paper she graded—the one she recalls using the misspelling. There it is, "Hunters and gardeners." And why did both students italicize the discussion questions? The spacing and structure are identical. In fact, the only

differences in the assignments are the students' names at the top of the page. They are the same paper!

Suddenly she began questioning the *B* she had confidently awarded the third paper. Who did this work? Student #3 or #10? Are they roommates? Have they both copied the paper from someone else? She wants to give them the benefit of the doubt, but should she?

How Millie Addressed the Problem

What this new online instructor now faces is the complex issue of assessment in the online world. This is, she is discovering, an area that requires the ability to differentiate between deception and misunderstanding without the benefit of "real-world" contact. It involves a mixture of psychological skills, keen observation (in this case of the written word), and good instincts—indefinable things that cannot be taught in a technical orientation session.

In the online environment, instructors cannot observe facial expression, eye contact, or body language. They will not overhear revealing comments in a classroom or hallway from other students who think they are out of earshot. And they have few practical ways of confronting students, except by e-mail or phone.

Which student should our heroine contact first? Both? Millie decides that because Steven's assignment was submitted 10 minutes after Marcie's, it might be reasonable to assume the work is hers, then copied, renamed, and submitted a few minutes later by Steven. She decides to question him first, and go from there:

Good evening, Steven. Thank you for submitting your Week 1 assignment on time. You did a nice job with the definitions and the discussion. I saw that you left the section on "materials" blank. The materials used to produce art during this period were largely "found"—charred wood from fires, sandstone, granite that could be broken and smoothed with other rocks, or cave walls (such as those in France I mentioned in the lecture). Initially, metals were not being produced, which limited the extent to which existing materials could be manipulated (no metal tools), nor could metal be used for art itself.

However, I did notice that your paper was identical to Marcie's. Please let me know which of you produced this work. Until we can get this cleared up, I will be unable to give either of you a grade for this assignment and my policy is that, should you submit copied work a second time, you fail the course. Please visit with me about this as soon as possible. Millie King

Typical Responses From Students Confronted With Academic Dishonesty

Rather than present a single scenario, the following are a selection of typical student comebacks. Anyone who has taught online for a year or two will recognize each of these and can probably add many more from personal experience:

Hi Ms. King. I have no idea what happened here. I did the work myself. Maybe they just look alike. I am not cheating or anything. Boy, I am really enjoying your class! It's so cool learning about the cave men and all their art.

Ms. King. Marcie is my girlfriend and we always study together and prepare papers together, because we are taking all the same classes this semester. We thought studying together was ok. We both did the work, but Marcie is better at typing, and I don't know how to submit to the Assignment Manager very well, so I need the help. But we both did the work. So can we study together or what?

I am a baseball player and I don't have time to submit everything. My coach will kill me if I take time from practice, and when there is a game I just don't have time. Sometimes Marcie helps me out by sending in my work—I guess it looks like she did it 'cause sometimes we work together. All of my

Online Resource on Plagiarism

Iowa State University's e-library site provides links to many tools and offers other excellent suggestions for addressing and preventing plagiarism:

www.lib.iastate.edu/commons/resources/facultyguides/plagiarism/detect.html

other instructors are friends with the coach, and they all understand that the guys on the team don't have time to do everything. It hasn't been a problem with them. Every other teacher is ok with it. I can't help it if I need some extra help from my roommate, or if I'm late with the work sometimes. My coach says ball players usually don't have to and there is nothing I can do about it.

Dear Mrs. King, I am international student from Turkey and have trouble still with English. I have lots of trouble with writing. My friend Marcie helps me put words on paper. She is helpful, and I don't know if I am able to do assignments without her. This is why our papers look the same. I am working hard in this course. I am having much trouble keeping up with my work, and I cannot afford the Intensive English program the college has. Is it not allowed for Marcie to help me?

Sorry Ms. King, I accidentally submitted my roommate's work instead of mine! I guess I was just tired from all the work I did this week, and I have been sick, and may even have to go into the hospital to see what is wrong with me. I think I am overworked with all these really hard classes! (ha ha!) Is it ok if I just change the paper and resubmit it so it doesn't look like the first one? Will I still get credit since it's not my fault? My computer has been messed up too.

Encourage learning through project -and problem-based learning. Collaborate with students to develop ground rules for policies and procedures for your class. Post academic policies and consequences, and be sure that students are aware that they apply in online courses as well as in traditional classrooms. Provide resources for students who may need tutors or additional assistance.

—*Terri Langan*
instructional development and delivery
Fox Valley Technical College, Wisconsin

How Millie Resolved the Problem

Now Millie has to make some decisions about both of these students. Should she further the argument by contacting Marcie? Or could it be that Marcie was a victim, unaware that her work had been plagiarized? The fundamental concern is that she is not sure who did the work. Who can she believe? Is there really some sort of unspoken exemption for ball players that instructors just accept as "the way it is?" Wouldn't that be unethical? How can she ensure that the problem will not continue? Is it cheating, a misunderstanding, or a unique circumstance that should be considered? The most important questions are as follows: Are both students successfully learning what the course is supposed to be teaching? Are they being honest with their feedback?

Much of this sort of situational response comes down to common sense. Is it reasonable to let baseball players off the hook? Of course not. Consider the single mother with three kids and two jobs. Doesn't she deserve the same consideration as a ball player? And how is softening requirements for one person fair to the rest of the class, some of whom have life complications that may exceed those of the player but remain unspoken. The bottom line is that when a student enrolls in your course, it is essentially an agreement between you and the student that there

will be good instruction and credit awarded if the student meets the requirements of the course.

Every student should be held to the standards set forth in your course syllabus and by institutional policy, which should clearly define not only the course requirements but also policies on academic honesty. There are, of course, a few special circumstances from time to time that will require some variance, but those times should be the exception, not the rule.

So, how does our new online instructor react to this situation and these student e-mails? As we already mentioned, every case is unique, and there are no pat answers. But Millie is an educator at heart, as well as a student advocate. She keeps in mind both her professional responsibilities and her students' success. She also keeps in mind the students' motivation. Are they trying to cheat, or is it a legitimate misunderstanding? She realizes that she must contact Marcie immediately with the same concerns. The following are examples of how Millie might then appropriately reply to three of the student responses previously mentioned:

Steven: Your papers are identical. I do not award any credit for copied work. In the future, I must have evidence that you and Marcie are doing your work individually, as

To prevent academic dishonesty, you sometimes have to save the students from themselves. Thinking like they do can lead you to establishi failsafe practices to guard against cheating. For example, if your students are taking a multiple-choice quiz for credit online, you might want to withhold the release of scores for all students until the class deadline passes, to ensure that no answers are shared between members of the cohort.

—*Susan Holmes*
online communications instructor
NorthWest Arkansas Community College

I cannot assign multiple grades to what appears to be a single effort. My policy is that if I receive identical documents, both receive failing grades until I have a chance to discuss the issue with the students. You need to see me about this immediately. Thank you very much for your help with this. I look forward to meeting with you about this paper and your next assignment. Millie King

Steven: I know you are busy, and you are having a great season! But I have a responsibility to the college to hold all my students to an equal standard. My policy is that if I receive identical documents, both receive failing grades until I have a chance to discuss the issue with the students. Thank you very much for your help with this. I know you can do as well in this class as you do on the ball field. I look forward to meeting with you about this problem, and to reviewing your next assignment. Millie King

Steven: It is great that Marcie is helping you. I have worked with international students and know it can be quite a task preparing assignments when your English skills are still developing. However, it is necessary for me to receive your work independent of Marcie. My policy is that if I receive identical documents, both receive failing grades until I have a chance to discuss the issue with the students. Please arrange to come see me about this immediately. Next time, please submit your own work, in your own words. I believe I will be able to understand your meanings and will e-mail you if I have questions. I hope to use this information to help you bet-

> **Teaching Tip**
>
> In English class, I use a few open-book quizzes, but mostly I evaluate students on written assignments. I usually give them practice assignments that are similar to major assignments and give feedback on the practice assignments appropriate to direct their efforts on the major assignments.
> —*Jane Schreck*
> *online English instructor*
> *Bismarck State College, North Dakota*

ter your English skills with some extra commentary and advice. Good luck! I am sure you will do well in this class. I look forward to your next assignment. Millie King

Whichever response the instructor decides upon, it is imperative that the student is made aware that the ramifications are potentially severe. Besides the very real possibility of failing the course, he or she could be subject to expulsion.

Where the situation goes from here depends on what happens during the next week. In most cases, students will recognize that they do have to submit independent documents and will comply. If they don't, our best advice is: Stick to the syllabus, stick to what you said you would do, and let the students bear their responsibility, as you have yours. And as was pointed out earlier, keeping a close eye on submitted work is imperative. Changing the format or wording of assignments each semester, having students work in varying group situations, and speaking directly with students when there are reasons for suspicion are all effective methods of limiting cheating or plagiarizing in an online setting.

CHAPTER 13

Knowing the Law and Following It

In this chapter, we examine legal issues encountered by online faculty and students, such as copyright, fair use, and other proprietary rights questions. We discuss protecting the rights of students, particularly as they relate to FERPA, and illustrate how the online environment creates confidentiality issues that may not be common in the traditional classroom.

Serving as an online instructor for a community college carries with it a responsibility for making sure the learning process you develop and carry through does not, simply put, break the law. Although all educators must adhere to legal behavior, online instructors face a unique challenge. Because we are so dependent on Internet resources, we are obliged to be particularly diligent in the appropriate selection or transfer of Web-based materials. As we identify appropriate legal behavior for online instructors (and students too), it is best to start by focusing on the concept of intellectual property.

We have all heard the lament of so-called Internet radicals who demand free information, proclaiming that the words and art of everyone should be community property and free for the taking. This notion has as much ethical merit as the arguments of those who defend shoplifting by lambasting the bureaucracy of big corporations. Property is property, tangible or not, and it presumably has value. Therefore, online educators need to be careful not to take what is not legally theirs. However, the reality is that there are vast gray areas that few people fully understand, and it can become a guessing game

determining whether some Web source can be legally used for your class. What exactly is intellectual property? Is it protected under copyright law or not? What about fair use? How about students' work—is that protected too? And the instructor's intellectual property? Does an online course belong to the instructor or to the institution?

This chapter is designed to provide you with a bare-bones overview of what you should consider before posting information to your course or before making your students' work or other information available to the public. This information should give you a starting place for at least knowing what to watch for. To find out more details, several good legal sites with specific information are provided.

What Is Copyrighted and What Is Not?

A copyright has two main purposes, namely the protection of the author's right to obtain commercial benefit from valuable work and, more recently, the protection of the author's general right to control how a work is used. Unless there is a clear statement that art, photos, and text are in the public domain and available for free use, the best policy is to assume

Ascertaining Fair Use: A Practical Example

Situation: One of your online students finds some great photographs during an Internet search and downloads them to incorporate into a multimedia presentation she is developing for your online English class. Is this legal under the fair use provisions of the copyright law?

Response: Use of the photographs by the student for class purposes is clearly within the limits of fair use, because they are being used solely for class information, education, or critique.

Situation: It is an outstanding report, and now you want to nominate the production for publishing on your institution's Web site. May the found photographs be legally incorporated? Under what conditions?

Suggestion: If the project is posted to the college Web site, it moves the use into gray areas and may require the copyright holder's permission. Look over the four criteria and the guidelines presented in the fair use section. Will you be making many copies? Will it involve a large amount of the copyright owner's work? (You should always assume it is copyrighted unless you know otherwise.) Will you be diminishing the value for the owner in any way? If you answer "No" to all of the questions, you are probably free to post the work. Nevertheless, the best rule of thumb is, if there is any doubt, get permission.

that they are copyrighted and should not be taken and used for republication on a local area network, a wide area network, or a Web site. If you are not sure, get permission to use the material first. The good news is that you will find that most owners of Web information respond positively when you plan to use something in an educational context.

Web pirates argue that work is not legally copyrighted unless there is a clear notice posted on the Web page or site. This is incorrect. Copyright law can protect work even if no papers have been filed with the government. Attorneys generally agree that students may use most copyrighted items for school reports, which go no further than the grade book. However, some companies can be extremely aggressive about anyone using their icons and logos, especially if their use is attached to anything less than complimentary. So caution is always advised. If you contact the copyright owner and permission is granted, it is still very important to provide a credit line near the item or at the bottom of the page and a complete citation of the source.

Today, protection for producers of information, including Web material, begins the moment that a work is fixed in a tangible medium. This protection is automatic. One need do nothing to secure it—no

registration and no notice requirement. Before 1978, the term of protection began when a work was published with the proper copyright notice. Works published between 1923 and 1978 were protected for 95 years, but works published after 1978 have a different term: the life of the author plus 70 years. An author's exclusive rights include the right to make copies; create derivative works; distribute, display, and perform works publicly; and authorize others to exercise the author's rights. Certain artists also have rights of integrity and attribution—our version of "moral rights" (Harper & Bruenger, 2005).

What Is Fair Use?

Fair use is a legal attempt at a balance of interests: It weighs the interests of copyright owners against the interests of the public, whose access to the works and the ideas in them can serve the common good. Fair use is sometimes described as embodying First Amendment concerns. For example, one can imagine that copyrights could easily be used to thwart speaking and listening if the rights to use the information were intolerably rigid. Fair use provides some breathing room.

One of the best examples of this is an instructor's reliance on the idea of fair use to quote from some work in order to criticize or otherwise comment on it. No copyright owner can legitimately refuse to permit such use, because courts consider it fair use of the information, and it does not devalue the property for the owner. Therefore, it does not require the owner's permission.

Fair use is a limitation on the exclusive rights of the copyright owner. The roots of what we today refer to as fair use are well established in early English common law tradition. The "fair use doctrine" is a complex exception to the "limited monopoly" vested in authors by the U.S. Constitution and the Copyright Act. The guiding principle of the fair use doctrine is to make available, for limited purposes, reasonable public access to copyrighted works.

An old-fashioned and widely held notion is that fair use mostly has to do with making copies. But it is broader than that. It applies to

- Making copies of copyrighted works
- Making derivative works (e.g., digitizing slides)
- Distributing works, including electronic distribution
- Displaying and performing works publicly

Section 107 of the Copyright Act, titled "Limitations on Exclusive Rights: Fair Use," is the statutory codification of the fair use doctrine. This judicially developed concept strives to balance the public's need to know and be informed against authors' incentives to create. The copyright law contemplates that fair use of a copyrighted work without permission will be for purposes such as (1) criticism and comment, (2) parody and satire, (3) scholarship and research, (4) news reporting, and (5) teaching and that such fair use will not result in the infringement of a copyrighted work. As one may expect, authors and publishers usually take a restrictive view of the fair use doctrine, whereas users of copyrighted materials generally take a more expansive view.

Fair use, as set out in Section 107 has two parts. The first describes uses that are "typical," such as criticism, comment, news reporting, teaching (including multiple copies for classroom use), scholarship, and

research. This list is not exhaustive, however, and even a use that is listed may not be a fair use. That is because each proposed use must satisfy the second part of the statute, which specifies four factors to be considered in each case:

- The purpose and character of the use
- The nature of the copyrighted work to be used
- The amount and substantiality of the part used
- The effect of the use on the market for or value of the work

The statute uses a "weighing and balancing" approach that introduces a variety of options for judgment. It is quite possible for two legal experts to consider the same use and come to different conclusions about whether it is fair. This, in a practical sense, creates a huge gray area for both educators and legal experts.

The important thing to take from this is that fair use is not a blanket exemption for educators. It is an exemption that permits certain uses of certain works for certain purposes, taking into consideration the interests of the owner of the copyright. If a use is not fair use under either the guidelines or the statute, an educator still has choices. He or she can change the use so it is fair, if possible; use a public domain alternative; or get permission (McKenzie, 1996).

The University of Texas system offers an excellent site that suggests guidelines for instructors to follow relating to the issue. It provides specific information for educators regarding fair use by category (e.g., textual, performance) Here is the condensed set of guidelines the Texas system suggests to their online teaching staff (Harper, 2005).

1. Students, faculty, and staff may incorporate others' works into a multimedia work and display and perform a multimedia work in connection with or creation of class assignments, curriculum materials, remote instruction, examinations, student portfolios, and professional symposia.

2. Be conservative. Use only small amounts of other's works.

3. Don't make any unnecessary copies of the multimedia work.

Although these guidelines are an excellent gauge of what you can and cannot do, they still have gray areas, which simply means that, even if you comply with the list, you are not necessarily complying with the law. Therefore, the best policy, if you have any doubts about the inclusion of copyrighted materials in your class, is to get permission from the owner.

Assessing Internet Content

Evaluating Information Found on the Internet
www.library.jhu.edu/researchhelp/
general/evaluating

—Published by Sheridan Libraries, Johns Hopkins University, author Elizabeth Kirk discusses criteria by which scholars in most fields evaluate print information and shows how the same criteria can be used to assess information on the Internet.

Assorted Myths About Copyright Law

1. If it does not have a copyright notice, it is not copyrighted.

This was true in the past, but today almost all major nations follow the Berne copyright convention. For example, in the United States almost everything created privately and originally is copyrighted and protected whether it has a notice or not. You should assume that any original work is legally copyrighted and may not be copied unless you know otherwise. Old work exists that has lost protection without notice, but you probably should not risk using it unless you know for certain. A notice strengthens the protection, by making the reader aware, but it is

not necessary. If a work looks like it might be copyrighted, assume it is. This applies to pictures, as well. You may not scan pictures from magazines and post them to the Web, for example. The correct notice usually looks like this:

Copyright [date] by [author/publisher]
or
© [date] by [author/publisher]

The term "All Rights Reserved" used to be required in some nations but is now not legally needed in most places.

2. If I am not profiting from its use, it is not a violation.

This is false. Whether you charge anything for copyrighted material or make any profit can affect the damages awarded in court, but that is the main difference under the law. It is still a violation if you give away the information outside of the provision of fair use, and there can still be considerable damages if that action ends up hurting the commercial value of the property. There is an exception for personal copying of music, which is not a violation, although that does not include widespread anonymous personal copying (such as Napster). If the work has no commercial value, the violation is mostly technical and is unlikely to result in legal action. Fair use determinations may depend on the involvement of money.

3. My posting was just fair use, right?

The fair use exemption to (U.S.) copyright law was created to allow use for commentary, parody, news reporting, research, and education about copyrighted works without the permission of the author. Intent and damage to the commercial value of the work are important considerations. Are you reproducing an article from the *New York Times* to criticize the quality of the *New York Times* or because you could not find time to write your own story or didn't want your readers to have to register at the *New York Times* Web site? The first is probably a fair use; the second probably is not.

4. If you do not defend your copyright, you lose it.

False. Copyright is effectively never lost these days, unless it is explicitly given away. Some copyrights do expire under the provisions mentioned earlier.

5. If I make up my own stories, but I base them on another work, my new work belongs to me.

False. U.S. copyright law is quite explicit that the making of what are called "derivative works"—works based or derived from another copyrighted work—is the exclusive province of the owner of the original work. This is true even though the making of these new works is a highly creative process. If you write a story using settings or characters from somebody else's work, you need that author's permission.

6. Copyright violation is not a real crime.

False. In the United States, commercial copyright violation involving more than 10 copies and value of more than $2,500 was recently made a felony (Templeton, 2005).

Are There Exemptions for Online Instructors?

Under the concept of fair use, the rights of copyright owners are exclusive (meaning that only they may exercise them), but they are not unlimited. There are many provisions of the Copyright Act that place important limits on the owner's rights. Those of special importance to community college online instructors include the following:

- Section 107 permits fair uses of works for teaching purposes without the owner's permission (as described earlier).
- Section 108 permits libraries to archive works, to make copies for patrons, and to participate in interlibrary loan operations, among other things.
- Section 109 permits all of us to dispose of our copies of a work without regard to the wishes or the pocketbook of the copyright owner. This provision, called the first sale doctrine, is

the backbone of our public library system and one of the principal ways that copyright law achieves its purpose to facilitate public access to the ideas contained in copyrighted works.

- Section 110 permits certain educational performances and exhibits in classroom or in distance learning, among other things.
- Section 121 permits entities such as organizations who work with the visually impaired to make copies without permission where a copyright owner has not made any special versions accessible to the disabled.

Performance Rights

Copyright law provides educators with a special set of rights enabling instructors to display recorded or live performances in the classroom. These rights apply to any work, regardless of the medium. When the classroom is remote, however, the law's generous terms are radically diminished—almost to the point of nonexistence. The severe limitations on what can be performed in distance education have received a good deal of attention.

In 1998, Congress directed the Copyright Office to prepare a report recommending what should be done to facilitate the use of digital technologies in distance education. Reportedly, copyright owners, particularly the publishing and entertainment industries, were appalled by the recommendations, and many copyright owners opposed their implementation. In short, many legal questions still exist where the recording or reproduction of performance is concerned. Again, the best advice is this: If you are not sure you can reproduce performance materials for your class legally, you probably should not do so without explicit permission. The fair use exemption remains difficult to determine in this area.

One reason fair use figures so heavily in performance rights for distance educators, or any educators who want to enhance their classroom teaching with online materials, is that putting anything online requires making a copy of it. Performance rights only cover the actual performance, not making copies.

Resources on Intellectual Property Rights

Intellectual Property & Copyright Resource Collection
www.adec.edu/user/copyright.html

University of Texas System Office General Counsel
www.utsystem.edu/ogc/intellectualproperty/index.htm

FERPA:
Separated Parenting Access & Resource Center
www.deltabravo.net/custody/ferpa.php

FERPA Tutorial
www.sis.umd.edu/ferpa/ferpa_what_is.htm

What Is Ownership as It Pertains to Students and Instructors?

Student work is intellectual property too, and it deserves protection against piracy when the students are older than 18 years of age. A college has no ownership rights regarding intellectual property created by a student solely for the purpose of satisfying course requirements, unless the student assigns rights to the institution in writing or unless the assignment of ownership rights to the college was a condition for participation in a course.

The author of an original work, including an online instructor, usually retains ownership interest in his or her work. However, if the author is a member of the academic staff who works for hire, or if the author is a faculty member who has been given substantial institutional support (such as additional salary or release time) for the creation of material, the university may have an interest in the work. Authors wishing to retain an interest in part or all of their work under these circumstances need to make that part of their contract. An author can assign copyright to anyone by means of a written contract.

Interest in instructional materials, including online courses, is not absolute. For example, an author can retain interest in the content of his or her notes, lectures, and exercises in an online course, while at the same time the college has an interest in the course itself. This has multiple implications. To consider just one example, this might mean that an author could publish the same content in textbook format, but the college could offer the course with another instructor.

Because interest is not absolute, employees are advised to negotiate contracts with the college administration to establish who has what interest before they begin work on a course. Issues to consider while negotiating a contract include, but are not limited to, whether other faculty members or members of the academic staff will be able to teach a course that an author designed, whether an author can take that course with him or her when leaving the college, and whether he or she can publish materials used in the course in another format. When copyrightable instructional materials are produced with support from outside the college, the agreement with the extramural sponsor has to be taken into consideration in determining who has an interest in what (Harper & Bruenger, 2005).

Accessibility Issues

In addition to the intellectual property issues that are so critical to Web-based instruction, a number of other legal considerations must be taken into account when teaching online. The federal laws often referred to as "504," "508," and "ADA" protect people with disabilities from discrimination and promote equal access for them. But which laws affect Web-based instruction and your responsibility and liability as an online instructor? The following summaries may help you determine what is applicable.

- Section 504 of the Rehabilitation Act (1973) requires all employers and organizations receiving federal assistance to provide people with disabilities equal access to information, programs, activities, and services.
- The 1998 amendment to Section 508 of the Rehabilitation Act does not directly apply to

colleges and universities, but it does mandate specific conditions for Internet and Web accessibility that are used as guidelines in designing and creating federal agency Web sites.

- The 1990 Americans with Disabilities Act (ADA) applies the same general principle as Section 504—equal opportunity to participate in programs and services—but it extends the reach to private organizations and any state or local entities not covered under Section 504.
- Other laws, including Section 255 of the Telecommunications Act, the Individuals with Disabilities Education Act (IDEA), and the Assistive Technology Act (1998) or ATA may affect Web-based instruction and how institutions may use federal monies (University of Maryland, 2005).

If ADA-related questions arise, it is good practice to consult your college ADA specialist to help you. Legal issues are usually best left to the experts.

Family Educational Rights and Privacy Act

The Family Educational Rights and Privacy Act (FERPA), also known as the Buckley Amendment, is a federal law that protects the privacy of students' education records. The law applies to all schools that receive funds under an applicable program of the U.S. Department of Education. FERPA gives parents certain rights with respect to their children's education records. These rights transfer to the student when he or she reaches the age of 18 or attends a school beyond the high school level. Students to whom the rights have transferred are "eligible students."

The records protected under the act may include handwriting, print, computer, videotape, audiotape, film, microfilm, microfiche, or e-mails containing information directly related to the student, such as, but not limited to, the following:

- Scores and results on standardized tests and interest inventories

- Academic records from previous schools
- Degrees awarded
- Current academic work completed
- Grades and other faculty evaluations
- Applications for admissions
- Applications and other data related to financial aid
- Applications for employment
- Class rolls
- Letters of recommendation
- Academic advisor notes
- Attendance data
- Biographical and identifying information
- Medical data

"Directory information" is data contained in an education record of a student, which would not generally be considered harmful or an invasion of privacy if disclosed, such as the following:

- Student's full name
- Address
- Telephone listings
- Date and place of birth
- Major field of study
- Degrees and awards received
- Dates of attendance
- Most recent previous school attended
- Participation in officially recognized activities and sports
- Weight and height of members of athletic teams

Directory information can be provided to the public through a directory or in other forms, unless students have expressly requested that it not be released. It may never include the following:

- Social security number
- Student identification number
- Race
- Ethnicity
- Nationality
- Gender

To remain in compliance with FERPA, never

- Use the entire social security number of a student in a public posting of grades.
- Link the name of a student with that student's social security number in any public manner.
- Leave graded tests in a stack for students to pick up by sorting through the papers of all students.
- Circulate a printed class list with student name and social security number or grades as an attendance roster.
- Discuss the progress of any student with anyone other than the student and authorized college personnel (including parents) without the consent of the student.
- Provide anyone with lists of students enrolled in your classes for any commercial purpose.
- Provide anyone with student schedules or assist anyone other than college employees in finding a student on campus. (U.S. Department of Education, 2006)

Some FERPA considerations affect online instructors in particular. When returning graded assignments or other work, it is especially important to ensure that copies do not inadvertently get sent to the entire class. It is also wise not to use attachments to commercial e-mail systems such as Hotmail because these sites are not always secure. Graded information also should not be sent to generic e-mail addresses at the student's home.

Slander

Those placing information on the Web must always be on the watch for slanderous content. In the case of schools, the courts have held that slanderous reports in high school newspapers are grounds for damages. The school is expected to protect people from such damage by reviewing content. Given the reality that Web publishing may reach a global audience, the damages resulting from malicious publishing may far exceed those from the old-fashioned college publications that were limited to hard-copy distribution. However, slander issues are rare in community college online environments.

CHAPTER 14

Hybrids and Learning Communities

Hybrid courses integrate online components into more traditional classroom formats to shorten classroom time or to enrich the curriculum. Learning communities bring a cohort of students together, adding support to each student's learning. An online component can strengthen this community and acquaint students with computer-assisted learning while a strong support group surrounds them.

Two learning modalities have been receiving considerable attention in the literature and in practice in recent years: the hybrid course and learning communities. Durham Technical College's Teaching-Learning Center Web site's section on hybrid learning opens with a quote by Graham Spanier, President of Penn State, in which he says, "Hybrid Courses are the single greatest unrecognized trend in higher education today" (Durham Technical Community College, 2006).

Whether teaching online, in the traditional classroom, or both, you may want to consider the instructional values of hybridizing your courses or creating learning communities. We treat the two together in this chapter, because we are convinced that they work well in combination. Most of our attention is given to hybrid courses, because online instruction is the focus of this book. However, the methods and tools discussed in earlier chapters suggest that Web-based learning may be one of the more effective means of addressing the two most difficult challenges presented by learning communities: scheduling and coordination.

Hybrid Classes

Many online students, when asked for a preference, indicate that they would appreciate the opportunity to meet face-to-face on occasion. An international student studying in the United States put it this way:

> One of the most helpful parts of adjusting to my new home is to get around the city and see it for myself. Then when people tell me where they live, I can create an image of that part of the city, and I feel that I know even more about them. It is the same with this class. I wish I could put a face on the names I know—other than just a picture. I would like to hear a voice, see how they react, listen to them laugh. Then I would know who I am studying with. (O. Zhadko, personal communication, January 17, 2005)

For the reasons discussed earlier in the book, face-to-face meetings are not always possible. Although new technology such as webcams can

Teaching Tip

Interact in discussions and provide feedback on assignments within days, not weeks. Build community through interactive activities, projects, and assignments. Require group work and participate yourself; however, teach students team-building strategies before requiring group work. Give students opportunities to grapple with content and teach it to others in class.

—*Terri Langan*
instructional development and delivery
Fox Valley Technical College, Wisconsin

enable us to see each other, hear voices, and listen to laughter, the asynchronous necessity of the format still limits in-person interaction. The hybrid class can bring together the best of both worlds. In addition, we do not believe that the entire curriculum should be available solely online. It is critical that core general education courses be available in traditional formats for students who need the security and comfort of face-to-face interaction. We do believe, however, that every course could benefit from being a hybrid.

Terri Langan of Fox Valley Technical College sees hybrids as a good way to break into online instruction. "Start your online career here. Build on effective classroom strategies, add online content and activities a little at a time to build comfort levels for both you and your students" (T. Langan, personal communication, December 14, 2005).

Furthermore, if we accept the overwhelming body of research that supports the value of learning in collaboration, group work, and students teaching students, every course should be a hybrid course. Why should we waste valuable "seat time" with a lecture, film, Web search assignment, or student presentations, when all of that can be done asynchronously via an online course manager? Students can be assigned to read lectures as we have suggested for an online course, view other students' presentations before coming to class, and research a topic via the

Web or library links between sessions. In-class time is then fully available for discussion about the previewed material and discussions about presentations that have already been reviewed and to analyze and problem solve rather than gather information. Instructors can then post questions to a discussion board that become part of the expected preparation for the next session's discussion.

With the pressures many institutions are feeling on classroom space, hybrids provide a legitimate opportunity to reduce time in the classroom without compromising learning. The learning environment can be enhanced by drawing the best of Web-based instruction together with the social and pedagogic values of face-to-face learning. Classes can meet weekly for shorter periods of time with small group work, intensive research, and asynchronous discussion occurring between sessions. We envision a future, in fact, in which faculty would be hired as hybrid teachers as part of master planning that would include committing fewer resources to new classrooms and more to online class management and faculty training.

Virtually all of the elements of online presentation discussed earlier in this book can be applied to hybrid classes, but several deserve particular mention.

Course Management System Access

A number of colleges are now assigning an online section for every course on their course management system. This allows faculty to use as many features of the system as they find useful to hybridize their classes. If your institution has not adopted this practice, you should at least ask whether the IT staff could assign an online section to your traditional courses.

E-Mail Correspondence

Although many faculty in standard on-ground courses use e-mail to communicate with students, a hybrid format increases the level and quality of this interaction and creates a greater sense of learning community.

Posting Lectures

As mentioned previously, a substantial portion of most classroom time is consumed with information transfer, when it might more usefully be committed to analysis, synthesis, and application. Posting your lectures in easily readable or audio format in an online classroom site allows students to read or listen to the material before coming to class, which allows you to commit meeting time to processing that information. We have heard some faculty complain, "If I post my lectures, students won't feel that they need to come to class." This should be the case only if the posted lectures duplicate what they would be receiving in class and become the sole basis for assessment. If class time involves other graded activities that rely on having read text or lecture material in advance, posted lectures should not be a factor in attendance.

Teaching Tip

Introduce a complicated concept or task during an on-campus session and carry the topic forward to the online classroom. Offer site links that help students learn more about the concept and keep the conversation flowing by offering open-ended questions from students and inviting comments. Ask for information and ideas that enrich the collective learning experience, and wrap up with an in-class collaborative activity incorporating the students' online efforts.

—*Susan Holmes*
online communications instructor
NorthWest Arkansas Community College

Threaded Discussion

One of the more popular tools used by teachers of successful hybrid courses is a discussion that runs on the discussion board between classroom sessions. The discussion might focus on questions the instructor draws from the week's in-class activities or may be more free form, allowing students to develop their own question sets based on the previous week's readings and lecture. Students, for example, might be expected to post an entry on the discussion board that addresses one point that was unclear to them

about the week's topic or to post one insight that was particularly useful or interesting.

Web Searches and Exercises

The resources of the Web are almost endless, and a simple hybrid exercise is to have students research topics on the Web or complete exercises to supplement the information provided in the text and lecture. Every student can be expected to come to class with the exercise complete, equipped with summaries of Internet resources that add to the richness and complexity of the face-to-face discussion.

Group Work and Presentations

By dividing your class into work or discussion groups in your online classroom, you can expect members to meet as groups between classes to discuss or formulate questions, develop presentations, and process the previous week's material. In a math course, online study groups might meet in chat sessions, work through problems, or prepare short presentations on a proof or solution for the next class. Students also can share presentations (PowerPoint presentations, for example) with groups in the online classroom and submit critiques to the instructor. This saves valuable class time that is often consumed with a string of student projects.

Testing and Assessment

Do you still complain every term when you have to wedge those time-consuming unit tests into class sessions that you know should be used to present or review new material? Using the strategies outlined in chapter 12 on successful testing and evaluation techniques, move your testing into the online environment. Virtually all of the standard assessment approaches, including performance evaluation such as taped speech presentations, can be accommodated online.

Any of the tools, techniques, and tips discussed in earlier chapters that are applicable to online classes have value for hybrids. Your trick is to select and skillfully use those that best complement your teaching style and learning objectives.

A Hybrid Model

Writing in *Educause Quarterly,* Margie Martyn (2003) related the experience of Baldwin-Wallace College with hybrid courses and the instructional quality it added to the institution. Admittedly, Baldwin-Wallace is not a community college and is, in fact, a small selective liberal arts institution. Nevertheless, the lessons learned have application to any learning environment.

The Baldwin-Wallace experiment involved eight "converted" classes that were largely delivered online but involved an introductory face-to-face meeting, followed by weekly online synchronous class sessions. Otherwise, the courses were delivered much as an online class would be. The introductory face-to-face session was used to acquaint students with each other and with the course management system, provide a course outline, review expectations, and explain the challenges students were likely to face.

One hundred and seven students enrolled in the eight courses, and only one failed to complete—a rate significantly higher than in the college's equivalent on-ground courses. Quoting Martyn,

> The faculty members who taught the courses reported that students in the distance learning courses achieved learning outcomes at a level equal to or higher than the traditional face-to-face classes. As a part of the approval process through Curriculum Review, the major course projects for all courses offered in the first semester were assessed by outside assessors using a blind-review process. The scores for projects in the distance learning classes averaged between 10 and 12 percent higher than those written by students in the traditional lecture format. In interviews, each faculty member reported that projects produced by the distance learning students were superior. One faculty member responded, "All three of the projects produced by this class [distance learning] were superior to projects produced by the traditional format. The reason for this is

obvious. I was involved in the learning process on a daily basis. (Martyn, 2003)

Using Online Strategies to Build Learning Communities

The ability to maintain learning standards and reduce seat time makes hybrid courses the perfect format for establishing or enhancing learning communities. By definition, a learning community is

> any one of a variety of curricular structures that link together several existing courses—or actually restructure the curricular material entirely—so that students have opportunities for deeper understanding and integration of the material they are learning, and more interaction with one another and their teachers as fellow participants in the learning enterprise. (Gabelnick, MacGregor, Matthews, & Smith, 1990, p. 19)

They take advantage of the phenomenon we see in programs such as nursing, in which a group of students takes a series of courses together and works together as a team—mentoring and instructing each other—to establish a sense of collective identity, accountability, and reward. These communities provide particular value in that they develop social and intellectual support circles for their participants, take full advantage of the values of collaborative learning, and provide a means for integrating different disciplines into a meaningful whole.

Although it is not our purpose here to sell the idea of learning communities, an explanation of their value by one of the early proponents might be helpful. Patrick Hill, Provost of Evergreen State College, stated in his 1985 address to the first Conference on Learning Communities of The Washington Center for Undergraduate Education,

> Learning communities are the vehicle for responding to a whole cluster of fundamental ills besetting higher education today. The concept of learning communities is not a

rigid one; there are a great variety of ways in which learning communities can be conceived. There are seven different issues to which the learning communities movement is a response. The issues consist of mismatched expectations of students and faculty, an inadequate amount of intellectual interaction between faculty and students, and between students and students, the lack of relationship or coherence among most of the courses taken by the student outside his or her major, the lack of resources and opportunities for faculty development, the growing complexity and interdependence of the problems we face with our disciplines, the non-completion rate in colleges and universities which has reached alarming proportions, and the shrinking budgets, a professional reward system, and internal patterns of resource allocation which reinforce and perpetuate the dominance of all the previous six structural flaws. (Hill, 1985)

All of the so-called flaws mentioned by Hill continue in one form or another, and both learning communities and online education may be steps to a solution.

If we were to use the course examples provided as illustrations earlier in this book as the basis for a learning community, we might enroll a group of students in the same sections of world religions, art history, and an English composition course. They would be enrolled for a 9-hour block, with the course managed by instructors representing each of the disciplines. The faculty would coordinate sessions and learning activities so that as students discuss the roots of Islam in the religion section, they would be researching Islamic art and writing papers about how the faith has influenced artistic expression.

The obvious challenge in establishing learning communities for large numbers of community college students is scheduling. With the typical mix of working adults, traditional high school graduates who attend full time, and part timers who scatter

---

Teaching Tip

During the first week of the semester, ask students to introduce themselves to the class using the bulletin board feature of the course. Students may choose to discuss topics such as their interest in the subject matter, their reasons for taking the course online, their educational goals, their hobbies, and the like. This gives students the opportunity to get to know the other students in the class. More important, it is the first step in building an online community that will serve as their classroom.

—*Jennifer Strickland*
online mathematics instructor
Darton College, Georgia

---

their schedules between day and evening classes, working out a 9-hour block for students becomes a daunting task. This is especially true if all 9 hours must be in the classroom. Place the equivalent of 6 of those hours online, and the challenge becomes much more manageable.

Instead, have the course meet for 1 hour Monday, Wednesday, and Friday, with each faculty member leading the discussion for one session weekly. The religious studies teacher leads off on Monday, directing small groups in discussion about what the students have learned from their Web search on the five pillars of Islam. On Wednesday, the art history member facilitates group reviews by students of the PowerPoint presentations they developed during the week, demonstrating how Islamic art reflects abhorrence for idolatry. The English instructor works with student groups on Friday as they critique each others' paper drafts, due in 2 weeks, discussing art as a reflection of Islamic faith and culture.

One of the principle strategies of learning communities is to involve students as teachers—giving them shared responsibility for shaping and delivering content. As we noted earlier, this often can be accomplished more successfully in the virtual classroom environment than in face-to-face settings, because students are often bolder, less self-conscious, and more creative when provided with a bit of physical distance. To take greatest advantage of online time, however, outside work must be substantive and intense and should revolve around learning groups that meet in live chat or virtual classroom sessions at other times during the week, depending on schedules. Faculty can then use this out-of-class time to meet, coordinate, and refine future sessions; discuss issues that have developed as the course progresses; and determine how specific student needs can be met with tailored out-of-class assignments.

Online application to learning communities is not a panacea for all of the challenges facing this collaborative approach. However, by hybridizing the learning community, both the instructors' and students' time becomes more flexible, and the need to find large blocks of dedicated classroom space is greatly reduced. There will be a tendency to suggest that developing learning communities is a large enough departure from tradition by itself, without the addition of a Web-based component. However, our interest in all innovation is not simply to experiment with techniques but to develop more effective learning strategies. If these two innovations work best in combination, we should at least try them. The result might be the solution we are seeking.

Conclusion

Imagine a future in which classrooms, as we traditionally think of them, are no more than occasional meeting places for students—spaces to get together two or three times a semester if schedules and distance permit. During the rest of the term, students are connected 24 hours a day to classes through hand-held "information stations" that include videophone, fax, television, and computer. When the class meets synchronously, students see each other and the instructor on their screens and are able to speak as easily as if they were face-to-face.

Degrees and certifications in this cyberworld are still granted by an institution, but colleges and universities are part producers of courses and part archivists, transcribing credits that students accumulate from institutions anywhere in the world. Articulation has been simplified by universally available course descriptions, syllabi, and instructor vitas. Students who match predetermined admissions profiles are able to enroll in courses appropriate to their status at any institution that accepts students with that level of preparation. The college can confirm the students' standing through a universal postsecondary admissions database and post the received credit back to that file once a course is completed.

There are still, of course, colleges and universities that specialize in the residential experience and others that insist that the majority of course work be from them, provided by their faculty. However, both of these institutional types have gradually become a rarity, as other social outlets have replaced residential student life, and rigorous and exciting composite degree options have gained respect and credibility. Division I football and basketball have gone the way

of baseball's minor leagues, but they attract the same avid fans—still as the Tar Heels, Razorbacks, and Bruins. University research has begun to cluster into research centers where only the most productive researchers and projects receive funding from federal departments and private foundations.

There are still teaching faculty—as many as there have ever been—although every instructor or "course facilitator" is now at least a hybrid teacher, and many, if not most, teach exclusively online. A movement that began among talented retirees has formed collaborative partnerships that also call themselves colleges, creating online course offerings and their own catalogs, made available to more traditional institutions on a just-in-time basis. When these co-ops first appeared, they were used as fillers to allow institutions to add late sections and accommodate unexpected growth. But colleges soon recognized that scheduling could be virtually on demand, and residential faculty were greatly reduced. Faculty of all kinds now have access to an almost limitless catalog of course units and modules available as open-source material to be organized and modified as the teacher wishes.

And learning? The old Western Governor's University model—where students could bring lower-division credit together from multiple institutions, then sit for qualifying exams in all upper-division courses without formal class attendance—was simply ahead of its time. As teaching and learning became less organized around institutions, and as learning modules became openly available in virtually every subject and to every degree of sophistication, the most independent-minded among students saw little reason for faculty at all. They said, "give us your best learning assessments and if we can demonstrate that we have mastered the knowledge, developed the skills, and can demonstrate ability to analyze and apply, give us the credit and the credential." Kicking and screaming, higher education acquiesced, and the Universal Credentialing Standard (UCS) emerged and prospered.

Like all forecasts, this one is not completely accurate. To the degree that it is, many of us do not like what it means for education. Some will say, "It can't happen." But more than we want to admit, it already has. Consider for a moment that from a practical standpoint, the World Wide Web has been around only since the 1990s. Yet already, 90% of community colleges are delivering courses online, and we are nearing the point that 50% of our students are using this delivery method. Degrees delivered completely online are not only available but also readily available, and public law and accreditation policies are modified each year to give them greater legitimacy. What other major innovation in education occurred with anything near that speed? The online future is now!

This reality presents every teacher in higher education with three options: resist the movement and remain part of the traditional on-ground instructional generation; move begrudgingly into online instruction by transferring your lectures, notes, presentation techniques, and attitudes onto the Web; or seize the opportunity to become a pioneer in this still relatively unexplored and inviting frontier of learning.

Those of you who choose to be pioneers will shape what online learning will be and what future generations of inspired teachers will look back on as the founding principles of cybereducation. We are often reminded as teachers that we teach as we were taught, and the best of the current online generation are at this moment molding the best of the next generation. This book invites you to use it only as a beginning point—a way to introduce yourself to the almost endless possibilities of this teaching and learning application. We trust that once you have developed your basic course online, you will experiment, refine, learn from your online colleagues, and respond to feedback from students until you have created the most interesting and effective course possible.

A colleague of ours, Herb Schade, has been teaching physics and physical sciences at Crowder College in Missouri for more than three decades. He taught the parents of many of his current students and in some cases, the grandparents. Most days at or around noon, you will find Herb and the lunch crowd gathered around the same table in the Crowder cafeteria, discussing college affairs, talking politics, or debating some issue that someone brought to the table. Herb's colleagues would probably describe him as a traditionalist. He is an experienced and skilled lecturer, and he likes to manage his classes much as he did 30 years ago. But when online instruction was introduced at Crowder a decade or so ago, Herb decided that as department chair, he should at least try the new delivery method. If he found merit in it, he should try to model it for his department. He elected to put a section of his physical sciences course online.

We know about Herb's online physical sciences class more through one of his students than from him. The daughter of another friend registered for the course—her first class online and a dreaded science requirement. Her mother, an elementary teacher, was skeptical about the whole arrangement, aware of her daughter's aversion to science, and dubious about anyone's ability to deliver an interesting and rigorous physical science course on the Web.

Then Herb's online science kit arrived. It contained, along with a list of a number of common household substances and containers, all of the materials the student needed to conduct her experiments for the semester. As the course progressed, Herb's instructions talked the student through one fascinating kitchen tabletop experiment after another, opening the young woman to a fascinating and applicable world of science that she had never imagined.

"The course was so good and the experiments so interesting," our teacher friend related, "that we would all gather around the table each time Amy had one to complete, anxious to see what happened. She did well in the course, and the whole family learned a lot about physical science." The lunch crowd at Crowder would probably say, "If Herb can do it, anyone can do it." It is not that Herb is not an extremely talented teacher, but he places high value on many of the old ways. However, he also knows that good teaching is good teaching, in whatever form, and that a good teacher, given the opportunity to be creative, will find ways to help students learn. (Several of his teaching tips are included in this book.)

To the rest of you—if you are a good teacher, we say "Herb did do it, and you can do it too."

Become one of the pioneers who shapes that future of Web-based learning. Create, explore, experiment, and become a learner yourself. The students who will be moving in ever-increasing numbers to online courses are expecting greatness, and they expect it from you. Those who will be teaching online in that still uncertain educational future will need exceptional mentors and guides. This is your opportunity to become one of them.

References

American Council on Education. (2003, August). *Student success: Understanding graduation and persistence rates* (ACE Issue Brief). Washington, DC: American Council on Education, Center for Policy Analysis.

Armstrong, L. (2000). Distance learning: An academic leader's perspective on a disruptive product. *Change, 32*(6), 20–27.

Bangura, A. K. (2003, April 14). Discussing America's wars in the classroom. *ERIC,* p. 4. (ERIC No. ED482478)

Campus Computing Project. (2004). *Tech budgets get some relief: Cautious support for open source applications.* Retrieved July 12, 2005, from http://campuscomputing.net/summaries/2004/index.html

Carlson, S. (2005, October 7). The Net generation goes to college. *The Chronicle of Higher Education, 52*(7), p. A34. Available from http://chronicle.com/free/v52/i07/07a03401.htm

Carriuolo, N. (2002). The nontraditional undergraduate and distance learning. *Change, 34*(6), 56–61.

Chickering, A. W., & Gamson, Z. F. (1987). Seven principles for good practice in undergraduate education. *AAHE Bulletin, 39,* 3–7.

Clery, S., & Solórzano, B. (2006, September/October). Developmental education and student success [Electronic newsletter]. *Data notes, 1*(7). Available from the Achieving the Dream Web site: www.achievingthedream.org

Cohen, A. A., & Brawer, F. (2003). *The American community college* (4th ed.). San Francisco: Jossey-Bass.

Collison, G., Elbaum, B., Haavind, S., & Tinker, R. (2000). *Facilitating online learning: Effective strategies for moderators.* Madison, WI: Atwood.

Community College Survey of Student Engagement (CCSSE). (2004). *Engagement by design: 2004 findings.* Austin, TX: The University of Texas, Community College Leadership Program. Retrieved March 7, 2005, from www.ccsse.org/publications/CCSSE_reportfinal2004.pdf

Conte, A. E. (2000). *In loco parentis: Alive and well.* Encyclopedia Britannica Online. Retrieved September 1, 2005, from www.watir.org/res/locoParentis.htm

Cross, P. (1999). What do we know about students' learning, and how do we know it? *Innovative Higher Education, 23*(4), 255–270.

Draves, W. A. (2002). *Teaching online* (pp. 52–54). River Falls, WI: LERN Books.

Durham Technical Community College. (2006). *Hybrid classes: Maximizing resources and student learning.* Retrieved October 13, 2006, from http://courses.durhamtech.edu/tlc/www/html/Special_Feature/hybridclasses

Gabelnick, F., MacGregor, J., Matthews, R. S., & Smith, B. L. (1990). Learning communities: Creating connections among students, faculty, and disciplines. *New Directions for Teaching and Learning, 41.*

Gehring, T. (2000). A compendium of material on the pedagogy-andragogy issue. *Journal of Correctional Education, 51*(1), 151–163.

Harper, G. (2005). *Copyright and image management.* Austin, TX: University of Texas System, Office of General Counsel. Retrieved August 8, 2005, from www.utsystem.edu/ogc/intellectualproperty/image.htm

Harper, G., & Bruenger, D. (2005). *Legal issues concerning the use of copyrighted material online: What constitutes fair use?* Retrieved August 8, 2005, from http://music.utsa.edu/tdml/conf-VIII/VIII-Harper&Bruenger.html

Hill, P. (1985). *The rationale for learning communities.* Olympia, WA: Washington Center for Improving the Quality of Undergraduate Education. Retrieved October 15, 2005, from www.evergreen.edu/washcenter/resources/upload/rationale1.pdf

Hirner, L. (2006). *Quality indicators for evaluating distance education programs at community colleges.* Unpublished doctoral dissertation, University of Missouri.

Holmberg, B. (1986). *Growth and structure of distance education.* London: Croom Helm.

Hoyt, J. E. (1999, Fall). Remedial education and student attrition. *Community College Review,* p. 18.

Jeffries, M. (2001). The history of distance education. *Distributed Learning.* Available from www.digitalschool.net/edu/index.html

Joy, E. H., & Garcia, F. E. (2000). Measuring learning effectiveness: A new look at no significant findings. *Journal of Asynchronous Learning Networks, 4,* 1.

Kemp, W. (2002). Persistence of adult learners in distance education. *American Journal of Distance Education, 16,* 65–81.

Lapore, A. R., & Wilson, J. D. (1958). *Instructional television research project number two: An experimental study of college instruction using broadcast television.* Retrieved October 24, 2006, from ERIC database. (ERIC No. ED014224)

Lederman, D. (2006, October 9). Opening up online learning. *Inside Higher Ed.* Retrieved October 11, 2006, from www.insidehighered.com/news/2006/10/09/cartridge

Lewis, L., & Farris, E. (1995). *Remedial education at higher education institutions* (NCES 97-584). Washington DC: U.S. Department of Education, National Center for Educational Statistics.

LexisNexis Statistical. (2005). *Internet user forecast by country.* Retrieved October 18, 2006, from LexisNexis Statistical Web site: www.lexisnexis.com/academic/1univ/stat

MacLean, A. M. (1925). Twenty years of sociology by correspondence. *American Journal of Sociology, 28*(4), 461–473.

Martyn, M. (2003). The hybrid online model: Good practice, *Educause Quarterly, 1,* 20–21.

McKenzie, J. (1996). *Keeping it legal: Questions arising out of web site management.* Available from the From Now On Web site: www.fno.org/jun96/legal.html

Meyer, K. A. (2002). Quality in distance learning: Focus on online learning. *ASHE-ERIC Higher Education Reports, 29*(4), 1–121.

Moore, M. G. (1989). Three types of interaction. *The American Journal of Distance Education, 3*(2), 1–6.

Moore, M. G., & Thompson, M. M. (1997). The effects of distance learning. *ACSDE Research Monograph* (No. 15). University Park, PA: Pennsylvania State University, American Center for the Study of Distance Education.

Moriber, A. C. (2000). Inspiration? Personal attention? Are they decreasing? *Kappa Delta Pi Record, 36*(3), 101–103.

Mountain Empire Community College. (2006). *MECC fact book.* Retrieved August 18, 2006, from www.me.vccs.edu/ir/index.html

Muse, H. E. (2004). The web-based community college student: an examination of factors that lead to success and risk. *Internet and Higher Education, 6*(3), 241–261.

Nasseh, B. (1997). *A brief history of distance education.* Retrieved October 13, 2006, from www.bsu.edu/classes/nasseh/study/history.html

Oblinger, D., Barone, C. A., & Hawkins, B. L. (2001). Distributed education and its challenges: An overview. In *Distributed education: Challenges, choices, and a new environment.* Washington, DC: American Council on Education and Educause. Retrieved August 18, 2006, from www.acenet.edu/bookstore/pdf/ distributed-learning/distributed-learning-01.pdf

Osborne, V. (2001). Identifying at-risk students in videoconferencing and web-based distance education. *The American Journal of Distance Education, 15*(1), 41–54.

Paredes, R. A. (2005, January 27). *Commissioner's report.* Presented at the meeting of the Texas Higher Education Coordinating Board. Retrieved October 4, 2006, from www.thecb.state.tx.us/Commissioner/ CommRep0105.pdf

Parsons, T. S. (1957). A comparison of instruction by kinescope, correspondence study, and customary classroom procedures. *Journal of Educational Psychology, 48,* 27–40.

Pascarella, E. T., & Terenzini, P. T. (1991). *How college affects students* (pp. 5–52). San Francisco: Jossey-Bass.

Paulsen, M. F. (1992). *From bulletin boards to electronic universities: Distance education, computer-mediated communication, and online education* (ACSDE Research Monograph No. 7). University Park, PA: Pennsylvania State University, The American Center for the Study of Distance Education. (ERIC No. ED354897)

Phillippe, K., & González-Sullivan, L. (2005). *National profile of community colleges: Trends and statistics.* Washington, DC: Community College Press.

Saba, F. (1988). Integrating telecommunication systems and instructional transaction. *The American Journal of Distance Education, 2*(3), 17–24.

Saettler, P. L. (1968) *A history of instructional technology.* New York: McGraw-Hill.

Sanderson, A., Phua, V. C., & Herda, D. (2000). *The American faculty poll.* Chicago: National Opinion Research Center. Retrieved November 2, 2006, from www.norc.uchicago.edu/ online/tiaa-fin.pdf

Templeton, B. (2005). *Ten big myths about copyright explained.* Retrieved August 8, 2005, from www.templetons.com/brad/copymyths.html

U.S. Department of Education. (2006). *Family Educational Rights and Privacy Act (FERPA).* Washington, DC: Family Policy Compliance Office. Retrieved January 2, 2006, from www.ed.gov/policy/gen/guid/fpco/ferpa/ index.html

University of Maryland. (2005). *Accessibility in distance education: A resource for faculty in online teaching.* Retrieved August 8, 2005, from www.umuc.edu/ade

Verduin, J. R., & Clark, T. A. (1991). *Distance education.* Oxford, UK: Jossey-Bass.

Watkins, B. (1991). *The foundations of distance education: A century of collegiate correspondence study.* Dubuque, IA: Kendall/Hunt.

Wheeler, S. (2002). Student perceptions of learning support in distance education. *The Quarterly Review of Distance Education, 3*(4), 419–429.

Glossary

andragogy The art and science of teaching adults.

asynchronous Not at the same time. Much of online teaching is asynchronous, because instructors and students read or post information when they have the opportunity rather than at the same time.

bandwidth The rate at which a computer is served by its connection to the Internet. High-bandwidth connections make audio and video files easy to download. Low-bandwidth connections are suitable only for text or limited multimedia use.

bookmark A feature that allows users to save their favorite Web sites (or ones they want to go back to) on a list so that they can find them quickly.

chat room A metaphorical room (window) where people can log on and post messages. Along with the displayed message, there is typically a message box where responses can be posted.

copyright A copyright has two main purposes: the legal protection of the author's right to obtain commercial benefit from valuable work and, more recently, the protection of the author's general right to control how a work is used.

course management system A software program that contains a number of integrated instructional functions, such as announcement boards, discussion rooms, and grading systems. These are also known as online delivery systems or platforms.

dialup access Refers to using a modem and telephone line to gain access to the Internet.

discussion board A form of chat room that is typically included as a regular part of online courses. The instructor has a space to type in a discussion forum, then there are message boxes where students can respond. Everyone in the class can read the messages, but they are usually posted asynchronously.

distance education Refers to teaching something from a distance, rather than in person, such as correspondence courses, teleconferencing, or online classes.

download To transfer a file from some remote location to your own computer.

electronic mailing list A list of addresses used for sending e-mail to a group of people simultaneously. *See also Listserv*

fair use The ability to use intellectual property to a limited degree for the purpose of teaching or discussion, without the permission of the copyright holder.

FERPA The Family Educational Rights and Privacy Act, also known as the Buckley Amendment, is a federal law that protects the privacy of students' education records. The law applies to all schools that receive funds under an applicable program of the U.S. Department of Education.

filters Software that reviews and blocks incoming material designated as inappropriate.

forum   A statement or question presented at the beginning of a discussion to stimulate and guide the discourse.

GIF   Stands for graphics interchange format. It is a compression format often used for graphics files that have a limited colors.

home page   The entry point, or first page, of a Web site.

HTML   Hypertext markup language, which governs the format of text and graphics on the computer screen.

hyperlink   A hyperlink, commonly referred to as a link, is a word in the text, an icon, or other particular spot on the screen that does something when you click on it with the mouse. Usually it connects the user to another Web site for additional information, or it might activate an audio file or digital movie that relates to the subject.

hybrid   A course that combines online and traditional in-person teaching.

icons   Graphic symbols representing programs, tools, or activities; they are often tied to the program or tool with an active link.

intellectual property   Refers to the legal protection given to the creator of written, artistic, or performance materials.

Internet   An electronic communications network that connects computer networks and facilities internationally. *See also World Wide Web*

ISP   Internet service provider; an organization (such as AOL) that provides customers with access to the Internet.

Javascript   This is a program designed to work with HTML to make Web pages interactive.

JPEG   An acronym for joint photographic experts group; a compression format used for photographs.

link   *See hyperlink*

Listserv   A trademarked software program for managing e-mail transmissions to and from a list of subscribers. When referring to e-mail sent to groups via a program other than Listserv, the more generic term *electronic mailing list* should be used.

local area network (LAN)   A network of interconnected computers in some small geographic area, such as computers in an office or on a campus.

modem   A device that allows a computer to receive and send information through a telephone or cable line.

multimedia   A reference to using more than one type of media, such as a combination of graphics, audio, animation, or video.

online delivery system   *See course management system*

open source   Information, programs, or systems available to anyone through the Internet at no cost and open to contributions and development by users.

operating system   The software that controls a computer and allows it to perform the most basic functions.

pedagogy   Originally referred to the science and practice of teaching children, but it also refers to teaching in general.

platform   Refers to the system your institution uses for the transmission of online courses, such as Blackboard, WebCT, and others. *See also course management system*

PDF Portable document format; produces files that can be read by different operating systems. Adobe Acrobat software both creates and reads PDF files.

plug-in An application that acts as a supplement for a Web browser and activates automatically when it is needed.

rich text format A data protocol for exchanging files between word processors. A format often used for the exchange of information in online courses, because it has low compatibility problems when transferring documents between computers. Files saved in this format end in the extension .rtf.

server *See Web server*

software The programs, routines, and symbolic languages that control the functioning of the hardware and direct its operation—instructions for the computer.

spam Unsolicited, usually commercial, e-mail sent to a large number of addresses. Also called junk mail.

streaming media Audio or video files that are sent from a Web site or other source in a continuous stream to the receiving computer. A software "player" program allows the content to be viewed or heard in real time.

syllabus A document prepared to describe, in detail, what work is required in a given course, how it is to be produced, and according to what timeline, along with institutional policy, required texts and materials, and method of assessment.

synchronous Happening at the same time, such as instant messaging or chat rooms when people are talking in real time.

threads Online comments made in relation to some subject that has been introduced in a discussion forum.

upload Transferring an electronic file from your computer to some remote computer.

URL An acronym for uniform resource locator; an address for a site on the Internet or World Wide Web.

virtual classroom An online location where instructors and students can meet and learn.

Web *See World Wide Web*

Web browser Refers to a software program that allows you to view and interact with the World Wide Web, such as Internet Explorer.

webcam A stationary camera focused on someone or something that broadcasts the picture live to computers.

Web server Software that functions to disseminate Web pages across the Internet; may also refer to the computer on which the software has been installed.

Web site The location where something (like teaching) takes place. It usually includes a number of pages, including text, video, audio, or links to other Web sites.

whiteboard A place where students can post messages to a common area visible to the whole class; functions much like a traditional chalkboard.

World Wide Web (WWW) Also called the Web, a part of the Internet accessed through a user interface and containing documents often connected by hyperlinks. Not every document on the Internet is available on the Web. *See also Internet*

Sample Materials for Online Instructors

In this appendix, you will find materials developed by online instructors for use in their courses: precourse letter, syllabus, instructions for using Blackboard, agenda, lecture discussion and questions, and project guidelines. They are provided as models or templates to assist you in developing your own course materials. You may adapt them to suit your purposes.

Precourse Letter

Dear [Student's Name]:

I am delighted that you have enrolled in World Religions, and I want to provide some early information about the course to give you a good start. As you are aware, this is an online class and will have no scheduled face-to-face sessions. Therefore, it requires a different kind of preparation than does a traditional course.

First, let me introduce myself. I have been teaching this course online for 6 years, and I love the subject! I live on a small farm (50 acres) west of town and play at being a farmer. My wife teaches, and we have two sons, one of whom graduated from the college last year. We like this area very much, and I enjoy being part of the college family. Next, let me give you some information about how the class will work.

Getting Into the Class

Our "classroom" will be the course Web site on the college's WebCT system. Because you are registered, you have WebCT access, but you may not know how to log on. For instructions, go to [provide Web address for logging on to the college's online platform].

Getting Your Books

You will not be loaded into the course by the Information Technology staff until August 15, so you can't explore the Web site before that time. However, you can purchase books for the class. We will be using two texts and will read all or most of both.

- Smith, H. (1991). *The world's religions: Our great wisdom traditions* (rev. ed.). New York: HarperCollins.
- Novak, P. (1994). *The world's wisdom: Sacred texts of the world's religions.* New York: HarperCollins.

These books are available from online publishers such as Amazon.com and barnesandnoble.com for approximately $34 new and as low as $4 used. Students also may want to check availability and prices with other online booksellers. The book may also be ordered from the CommCollege Bookstore using a credit card—by calling 555-455-5588 between 8:00 am and 7:00 pm Monday–Thursday or 8:00 am to 4:30 pm Fridays or by logging onto the bookstore's site at www.commcollege.edu/bookstore.

Read the Syllabus

This week, I will be sending you a lengthy e-mail describing how to initially navigate the class Web site. A copy of the course syllabus will be attached. Please copy and save this e-mail message and the syllabus until you can access the course site, because they provide initial instructions.

Start Date

We start August 22. Log into the class that day or before to begin work.

Technology Needs

You will need a computer that has the capability of playing video clips. If you have Windows XP or a similar Windows edition, it will include Windows Media Player, which will do the job. Because you will be downloading these 3- to 10-minute clips, you will also want a high-speed connection to the Internet or access to it through another computer. If you are using dialup, you will want to go to the college or another location where there is a high-speed connection. ***Please let me know right away if you will be using dialup connectivity to the Internet as your primary access***. I may be able to make the video clips available to you on a CD.

Check E-mail

Check both your personal and college e-mail accounts. For class purposes, we will be using the college e-mail addresses. I will make the technological elements of the class as simple and transparent as I can. In addition to learning the subject matter, another value of this course is that it can increase your ability to use technology. We will have a fun time and learn a great deal. I'll "see" you in class on the 22nd!

Yours truly,
[Instructor's Name]

Syllabus

Course Title:	Philosophy 121—World Religions
Instructor and Course Designer:	Willard Witt
Course Credits:	3 credit hours
Phone:	1-555-455-5534
e-mail:	wittw@commcollege.edu
My Web site:	www.commcollege.edu/directory (select my name under "faculty and staff")

Course Web Site: http://blackboard.commcollege.edu

When you enter this Web site, you will find a login prompt for your user name and password. Once logged in, this course number should appear on your course menu. If not, you are not yet formally registered. Please contact the registrar's office at 555-455-2171.

Computer Tech Support for Online Classes

If you have network or computer compatibility problems, please call Tech Support at 555-455-5712.

Help Information for Using Blackboard

Log into the class Web site and select Tools from the menu on the main page. You will find a Student Manual choice here that has a very good index of help topics.

Introduction

Welcome to World Religions! If you allow yourself to approach this class with an open mind and intellectual curiosity, you will find the subject to be one of the most fascinating you will encounter during your college experience. This class will broaden your understanding of the world, its peoples, and yourself. It will help you relate major developments in human history and will give greater meaning to current events. In fact, you may come away from this course convinced that the major religions of the world are the single most important contributor to thought and action and, therefore, to the course of human events.

Catalog Course Description

Students compare and survey the great world religions, emphasizing concepts of God, creation, the human race, scripture, ethics, and salvation. This rational analysis concentrates on Hinduism, Buddhism, Jainism, Confucianism, Taoism, Shinto, Zoroastrianism, Islam, Judaism, and Christianity. Students successfully completing this course partially fulfill general education requirements in either the humanities or social sciences, but not both simultaneously.

Course Goals

Through this course, students will gain an understanding of and appreciation for religions and will recognize the influences these religions have on who we are, how we think, and how we relate to others.

Performance Objectives

Students successfully completing the course will be able to

- Explain why it is important to the average person to know what the major religions of the world believe.
- Describe how history has influenced each religion's development and how each religion has influenced history.
- Explain the major ideas that shaped each religion's development and how modern ideas are affecting each now.
- Describe how a religion is influenced by where it began and where it is now dominant.
- Outline how each religion has changed in beliefs and practices over time.
- Describe and distinguish between the philosophical, moral, and ethical elements that make each religion important to its followers and to the student.
- Design a model that illustrates relationships among members of the major religious families.

Course Length and Format

The course will be divided into five 2- to 3-week seminars, with approximately 8–12 hours required each week to successfully complete the course. *It is very important that you have at least the minimum amount of time to devote to this course during each of the 16 weeks.*

Prerequisites

Students will need a minimum of the computer hardware and software indicated in the CommCollege Online Orientation, Internet access, and e-mail capabilities. In terms of previous course work, this course has no formal prerequisites, but because it is very reading- and writing-intensive, students will benefit from having completed a college-level writing course and from having good reading comprehension skills.

Texts

- Smith, H. (1991). *The world's religions: Our great wisdom traditions* (rev. ed.). New York: HarperCollins.
- Novak, P. (1994). *The world's wisdom: Sacred texts of the world's religions.* New York: HarperCollins.

These books are available from online bookstores such as Amazon.com and barnesandnoble.com for approximately $34 new and as low as $4 used. Students also may want to check availability and prices with other online booksellers. The book may also be ordered from the CommCollege Bookstore using a credit card—by calling 555-455-5588 between 8:00 am and 7:00 pm Monday–Thursday or 8:00 am to 4:30 pm Fridays or by logging onto the bookstore's site at www.commcollege.edu/bookstore.

Biweekly or Triweekly Sessions

Seminar 1   Introduction to the online format, to the nature of religion and to the world's religious families; discussion of Native American and African tribal religions

Seminar 2   The religious family of the Indian subcontinent: Hinduism, Jainism, Buddhism, and Sikhism

Seminar 3   The religions and philosophies of East Asia; religion in ancient China/Japan: Taoism, Confucianism, and Shinto

Seminar 4   The religious family of the Near East: Zoroastrianism and Judaism

Seminar 5   The religious family of the Near East (continued) Christianity, Islam, and developments of the last two centuries.

Time Requirements

Every participant is different, but this course is designed to require 8 to 12 hours per week for 16 weeks. This is an intensely interactive course that depends on dialogue and discussion to achieve the learning outcomes. You are expected to log in and contribute a minimum of 4 times per week (although most participants log in almost daily). Many assignments require peer review and feedback, and your classmates need your regular input during the 16 weeks. If you fall more than a week behind on assignments, I may ask that you drop the course, because you will not be able to contribute to the ongoing discussion if you are too far behind.

Assignments

Specific weekly assignments with due dates are outlined in the seminar agendas that are posted under Course Documents on the main course menu. Copy these agendas for each seminar and refer to them for day-to-day assignment information.

Personal Biography. During the first week you are asked to post a biography of yourself (see the agenda for Week 1).

Readings. Each week there is a reading assignment from the texts or other supplemental materials. To encourage you to keep up on the reading, a 10-point reading summary based on questions I give you will be an important part of your grade. Reading preparation is key to good class discussion and to understanding material presented in class.

Lecture Questions and Responses. Each week you will read a posted lecture and respond on the discussion board to questions that I post at the end of the lectures. During the latter part of the week, each student is required to critique the answers of at least two classmates, also on the discussion board. Initial answer postings are worth 20 points per week, and responses to classmates are worth 10 points per week. To receive full credit for your question responses, they must be thoughtful; at least one paragraph long; and reference material in the text reading, the lecture, or other supplemental information you find through your own research. Please cite the reference in your response.

Exams/Writing Assignments. There will be four 75-point exams or written assignments during the semester, totaling 300 points. The first exam will cover Hinduism, Buddhism, Jainism and Sikhism; the second Confucianism, Taoism and Shinto; the third Zoroastrianism and Judaism; and the final, Christianity and Islam. The exams will generally have three sets of questions to be answered in essay form.

Major Research Paper. Each class member will prepare a research paper (10 to 12 typed double-spaced pages) on some aspect of any of the religions discussed other than the religion with which you affiliate yourself. Look under Assignments on the main menu to find detailed information about paper topics, format, grading, and other expectations.

Net Pal. Part of your final grade depends on your corresponding with a person who belongs to the religious group about which you are writing your major research paper. You must find a Net pal with whom you can correspond during the semester and turn copies of your exchanges in to me every 3 weeks. This correspondence is worth 100 points during the semester or 20 points for each of five due dates. Look under Assignments for information about how to find a Net pal and how to initiate an online discussion.

Attend Service. You are required to attend a service of one of the religious groups we discuss, other than one with which you affiliate yourself, and write a brief summary of the proceedings. If you live close enough to take advantage of it, I have arranged visits to services at a synagogue, a Sikh temple, and an Eastern Orthodox church. Otherwise, you will need to find a service on your own.

Other Assignments. There are two other brief written assignments during the semester and an online search assignment (see Assignments site for details):
- Between our first and second session, each of you will conduct an Internet search to locate sites that can be helpful as you work on other assignments during the semester.
- Following the session on Buddhism, you will submit original haikus, a stylized form of Zen poetry, which will be discussed in class that week.
- The week of the final, I would like you to submit a short (2- to 3-page) essay addressing this question: How has studying the major religions of the world influenced my thinking about myself, other people, and the world I live in?

Academic Honesty

The work you turn in must be your own. I routinely check sections of papers to see if they are taken from other sources without proper credit. If you take written work from another source without showing where it came from, this is plagiarism, and you will not receive credit for the assignment. (See the college catalog, page 17, for its policy on academic honesty.)

Grading Criteria

Students will be graded on a point basis using the point totals for assignments shown below:

Personal biography	20
Weekly reading question responses	150
Response to lecture questions (20 each lecture)	300
Comments on classmate's answers (10 each)	150
Major exams (four at 75 points each)	300
Major research paper	100
Net pal correspondence (five at 20 points each)	100
Attend service	30
Internet search	30
Haiku	20
Short essay at end of course	30
Total	**1230**

20 extra credit points can be gained by attending a second service or by visiting a temple, mosque, or shrine of another faith. See the agenda for Seminar 1 for details.

A = 1107–1230
B = 983–1006
C = 859–982
D = 735–858

Instructions for Using Blackboard

About Blackboard

Blackboard is the main platform this college uses as an easy way to organize course materials for Web-based delivery and to facilitate participation with class members. We will be using eight or nine features of Blackboard on a regular basis, so it is important that you become comfortable with their use. I will give you a quick rundown on each, but you can learn a great deal more about Blackboard and its features by going to the main login menu, where you read my first announcement, and selecting Tools on the menu to the left. One of the choices under Tools is Student Manual. This manual will teach you all of the finer points of Blackboard. Here is a quick rundown of the major features we will be using.

Announcements

When you sign onto the college's Blackboard site and select our course, SOC 121, the opening menu will immediately display any announcements I have for you. Always look at Announcements when you log in to see whether anything new has been posted. I also will use the announcements to post observations about our discussion at the end of each week, so they will automatically appear when you enter the class site.

Course Information

You visited the Course Information site to find this document, so you have seen what choices are here. This is where I post information related to the course as a whole—the syllabus, how to use Blackboard, sample research papers, and the like. If I add anything new to this site, you will be notified in the announcements.

Course Documents

This menu choice is one of the two most important. Here you will find the course broken down into four seminars, each covering 3 or 4 weeks of the course. In each of these seminar folders is all of the information you need to complete assignments for the weeks covered in that seminar. The first item in each of the seminar folders is what I call the agenda. It outlines each week on almost a day-by-day basis, telling you what is due on what day and giving you a little warning about what assignments are coming up that you need to be thinking about. The lectures, film clips, and short supplemental readings for these weeks will all be in the folder for that seminar.

I have included a number of short film clips in the seminar folders. To play them, you will need something like Microsoft Media Player or another software package that allows you to view MPEG video. If you are connected to the Internet by dialup modem, loading these clips could take a long time. I suggest in that case you view these clips at a computer at the college or at another place with high-speed connectivity. As a last resort, I can make the clips available to you on a CD for the nominal cost of getting it recorded, but I prefer not to do this unless absolutely necessary.

Discussion Board

The Discussion Board choice on the menu takes you to a site where you can respond to the questions I pose at the end of each lecture contained in the seminar folders. When you get to Discussion Board, you will find Forums already set up. One is for you to post a biography, as instructed in Agenda 1 for the first week of class. The second forum that will already be there is called Week 1 Discussion. When you click on this choice, you will see a box that says Create a New Thread. By selecting this, you get a subject box where you can name your entry (e.g., Response to Question 1–1A) and then a larger box where you enter your answer.

Here are a few hints about using the discussion board. The large window boxes for your answers work just like a Microsoft Word window. You can create an answer on another page, copy it, and paste it into this window. You can then edit it, just like a Word document, or you can delete it and reenter if you wish. So, you do not need to create your answers in this box to begin with if you prefer to write them somewhere else.

Once you have made your entry and submitted it, it will show up on the Discussion Board with the title you have given your entry, your name, and the date and time you posted it. Other class members can then come to the discussion board, click on your topic, and read your answer. (If they click on your name, they get your e-mail address and an e-mail message box.) After reading your response, they can select Reply and type a response to your entry that will then appear below your entry, slightly indented, showing that it goes with your answer. This begins what we call a threaded discussion, with others being able to respond to the initial answer or to your response to it. Once you have posted a response, it is possible to go back and edit it, so you can change your responses if you think of something after the fact or wish you had not said something!

You will note that I have a forum on the discussion board called Sidebar Discussions. This is where I would like you to go when you want to have a discussion with other class members that does not relate specifically to the course topic for the week. You might type an entry on the main discussion forum that has as a subject, "see sidebar," letting people know that they do not need to read this as part of the class discussion for the week but that they may want to check it out. This cuts down on the amount people have to read to get through the discussion for the week if they do not want to participate in these sidebar discussions.

As protocol on the discussion board, this is a place to agree, disagree, challenge, and question but not a place to be rude, caustic, or seriously confrontational. It is a place of civil discourse, and I will regulate that if I see it getting out of hand.

Assignment Manager

The Assignment Manager under Assignments on the main menu allows you to leave assignments there, where I can grade them and return them to you directly through this location. It will be our standard method of exchanging assignments, unless I tell you otherwise on the agenda or in an announcement.

Communication

When you select Communication on the login menu, one of the choices will be Send E-mail. This site gives you a list of all of the class members with e-mail addresses, and you can select one, several, or all class members. You can also reach me through this menu choice.

An option to having a sidebar discussion is to send e-mail to class members. I will use this regularly during the semester to correspond with you, send assignment drafts back and forth on occasion, and so on. I need to let you know that there is a slight chance whenever e-mail is used to transmit documents that the document could be intercepted by someone else and looked at. I will therefore not send graded assignments back and forth using e-mail attachments; I will use the assignment manager for this purpose.

I will occasionally schedule chat sessions when we need to all be online at the same time. The collaboration selection under Communication on the main menu will direct you to the chat sessions. You will see the session scheduled at the time we have agreed on and simply have to click on join.

Communication is also the section where you will find groups set up. For some projects and assignment review, I will have you work in smaller groups. I will let you know when the groups have been established and who is in yours. You can go to the Communication site, select Groups, and find your group's forum. This feature allows you to communicate with each group member using group e-mail, to hold chats together, and to exchange information and materials just with your group if you choose.

View Grades

If you select Tools on the main menu, the last menu choice is View Grades. This choice allows you to go to a grade book where all of the assignments, including points for the weekly discussion entries, are entered. I am pretty good at keeping your discussion board participation points up to date, and as you can see, they are sufficient to affect a letter grade. The Grade Book keeps a running total of your points and shows what percentage of the total you have achieved at any point.

External Links

The External Links choice on the main menu takes you to a site where I have listed Web sites that supplement information in the course. By selecting these sites, you are taken directly to that Web site. You will see that in the lectures, I often have these links embedded right in the lecture, but External Links provides another access area for Web resources.

Agenda

Seminar 1:
The World's Major Religions:
Concepts, Terminology, and Organization

Unit Objectives for Seminar 1

In Seminar 1, we will become acquainted with each other as a class and will lay the foundation for our exploration of the world's major religions. We will become familiar with important terms that will help with later discussion and understanding and will begin to examine how the religions fit into "families" with common characteristics and connected origins. Using Native American and African tribal religions as a basis, we will determine whether all characteristics have to apply to all religions; this will give you a chance to see how the terms learned in this seminar apply to actual religious practice.

Seminar 1 also serves to acquaint you with the online techniques and assignment types I will use throughout the course. Reading the text is extremely important in that it provides necessary background for much of our discussion. Each seminar includes reading assignments as well as several lectures from me and from special guests. Read the text assignment and Lecture 1, respond to the questions, and complete the Internet search before you try to locate a Net pal. The readings, lecture, and Internet search will help you decide where (in what religious family) you want to look for an interesting paper topic and Net contact.

Print out the agenda for each seminar as it comes to you and use it as a reference guide and checklist for assignments. For this seminar, I will have forums available on the discussion board for each week, labeled "Seminar 1, Week 1—Tribal Religions," for example.

Upon successful completion of this seminar, you will be able to
- Describe the general characteristics of a religion.
- Organize the world's major religions into families and provide basic explanations as to why they are grouped as they are.
- Describe how the characteristics we have identified appear in Native American and African tribal religion.
- Use Internet resources to find information about each of the religions to be discussed and to find a Net partner from one of these religions.
- Provide examples of how religion is influencing relationships among peoples and nations today.

Assignment Posting

Unless otherwise noted, all assignments should be posted to the discussion board or to the assignments file (see Blackboard menu) rather than to me personally by e-mail.

Week 1

1. **Post biography/goals.**—*Due Friday, January 17, 5:00 pm*

   Prepare a brief autobiography using the questions listed under Bios in the Seminar 1 folder and post it to the bios discussion forum on the discussion board. Print out the bios from other students for quick reference.

2. **Read the Smith text.**—*Due Wednesday, January 15, 5:00 pm*
   - Read Smith, Introduction, Chapter 1 (pp. 1–30).
   - Write a brief summary addressing the following questions and send it **to me only** as an e-mail attachment (one or two paragraphs per response):
     - What thoughts did you have as you read these chapters about the nature of religion? Did you agree or disagree with the definitions?
     - What examples do you see in modern life and religion of some of the characteristics mentioned in the chapter on basic religion?

3. **Read Lecture 1A.**—*Due Wednesday, January 15, 5:00 pm*

   Read Lecture 1A and answer questions on the discussion board in Forum 1-A before completing Assignment 6. When answering a question, indicate "answer to question 1A" and so forth, so others will know what your response relates to. *Each answer must be a full paragraph of not less than 60 words to receive full credit and must meet the criteria listed in the syllabus. (See syllabus for instructions.)*

4. **Respond to the answers of at least two of your classmates.**—*Due by no later than Friday, January 17, 5:00 pm*

   Using the Discussion Board, Forum 1-A, respond in a paragraph or two to the lecture answers of at least two of your classmates. In the Subject box, label your response to indicate the nature of your comments (i.e., "about tribal religion"). Do not say simply "I agree" or "good thoughts"; provide detailed answers.

5. **Search the Internet and post a research summary.**—*Due Monday, January 20*

   Go to the Internet and find three separate sites that provide information about three of the religions we will study during the semester. Use the text to identify religions that might interest you. See "A Very Quick Web Tutorial" in the Course Information section if you are new to Internet searches. Post a 2- to 3-paragraph summary of each search, including how you located the sites, what the sites included, and your comments and opinions about their value: Do not just copy the information from the site. Send these paragraphs as e-mail messages or attachments to the whole class using the e-mail selection listed on the Communication menu.

6. **Find a Net pal.**—*Due Friday, February 7*
    You have 3 weeks to do this, so take a little time thinking about who you want to find. Look through the text and scan the chapters to see what religion might particularly interest you. Don't select something you are familiar with. Then locate a person who belongs to that religion who is willing to correspond with you by e-mail weekly over the next 14 or 15 weeks. In the Course Information section, you will find a sample introductory e-mail and some follow-up questions to get a discussion started. For help finding a Net pal, look at the External Links selection on the main course menu. I have listed some sites there that will help.

Week 2

1. **Read the Smith text.**—*Due Wednesday, January 22, 5:00 pm*
    - Read Smith, Chapters 2 and 3 (pp. 31–75).
    - Type and submit to me as an e-mail attachment a simple review of the reading, addressing the following questions:
        - Where do you see similarities in the African and Native American religions? Where are there differences?
        - These religions are sometimes referred to as *primitive.* Is that term justified? Explain your answer.

2. **Read Lecture 1B.**—*Due Wednesday, January 22, 5:00 pm*
    Read Lecture 1B and answer questions using the Forum 1-B on the discussion board. Remember that answers need to be substantive and to reference the text, lecture, or other material you have found.

3. **Read the faith essay by the Shawnee tribal member.**—*Due Friday, January 24, 5:00 pm*
    If your computer allows, view the video clip titled "Shawnee presentation" in the Seminar 1 folder.

4. **Respond to the answers of at least two of your classmates.**—*Due [date]*
    Using the "Discussion Board, Forum 1-B" respond to two of the lecture answers of your classmates. Remember to give your response a subject title that relates to what you have to say. These responses need to be more than "I agree," or "good thoughts," but good, thoughtful answers.

5. **Review the Web sites I have posted under External Links for contact ideas and resource information.**—*Due [date]*

Lecture Discussion and Questions

Leadership and Ethics

Introduction

In this week's lecture, we are going to take a very specific look at an issue that is a natural extension of our discussion about leadership: ethics. If leadership involves the exercise of power and its use in negotiating for and using scarce resources, misusing power and managing the system for unethical use of these resources must be an area of concern. In fact, if power and control are necessary for effective leadership, an opportunity for abuse of that power will always exist, and ethics is a discussion about the appropriate use of power, influence, and control.

The text mentions J. M. Burns' 1978 book, *Leadership,* as one of the commonly cited treatises on ethics. Lax and Sebenius, also mentioned in the text, use Burns's work as the basis for much of their own writing on the subject. They draw four rules from Burns for judging whether an action is ethical. Read the brief excerpt from Burns that I have included in a folder titled "Burns Reading" in the Seminar 2 folder, then think about each of these rules as you consider leadership decisions you see being made about you each week.

What Is Ethical?

To summarize the rules presented by Burns, when determining whether an act or decision is ethical, one must consider the following:

1. Mutuality: Is everyone operating with the same information and understandings?
2. Generality: Does the action being taken follow general standards of morality that would be applied in other similar situations?
3. Openness: Would you mind if your mother knew about this action or if you knew you would read about it in tomorrow's paper?
4. Caring: Does this action show caring for the legitimate interests and actions of others?

Note that there is nothing in these rules that talks about legality, and it is important to point out that there is a significant difference between whether something is legal and whether it is ethical. I am not going to provide examples here, because I want this distinction to be the basis for our questions on the discussion board, but be thinking of examples of cases in which something might be legal, but not ethical, and decide whether there might be cases in which something might be ethical but not legal.

Ethical Dilemmas

One of the interesting problems with ethics is that it often creates dilemmas that are not just matters of making a decision between what is right and what is wrong. Those dichotomous issues (those in which there is a clear right and wrong) generally suggest the proper choice. The more difficult ethical issues, the ones we might call "ethical dilemmas," are those created when the decision involves a "right versus right." Here I will give you an example.

Years ago, at another college, I had a colleague—one of our senior faculty in the Business Department—who was doing a terrible job in the classroom. He was trying very hard; he met with his classes regularly and prepared for hours, but he was becoming forgetful and confused in his presentation of material. Students were getting practically nothing from his classes. Our suspicion was that he was showing the first signs of Alzheimer's. He had 28 years with the college and had been one of its most loyal supporters, attending more student functions than practically any other faculty member, contributing regularly to the foundation, and accepting more than his share of committee assignments. Students loved him as a "friend and college champion," but they felt completely ill prepared in their introductory accounting courses, the mainstay of the curriculum. However, he could not retire with full retirement benefits for another 2 years.

Normally the simple answer would have been to find another assignment for him for a couple of years until he could fully retire, but the college became aware of the situation during the early years of one of the state's fiscal down cycles when departments were having to reduce budgets significantly and leave some vacant positions unfilled. It was difficult to justify hiring a replacement for a person receiving a full, and relatively high, salary when departments were going without. A "right–right" dilemma! It was right to keep this faithful and long-term faculty member employed, but it was also right to provide students with good instruction in a key area. So the dilemma was how to do both with no budget with which to do so.

Rushworth Kidder, one of the country's great ethicists and author of the books, *How Good People Make Tough Choices: Resolving the Dilemmas of Ethical Living* and *Moral Courage*, identifies four sets of circumstances under which these right–right situations might develop. These circumstances are

- truth versus loyalty
- individual versus community
- short term versus long term
- justice versus mercy

You can learn more about Rushworth Kidder and his thinking about ethics by going to www.globalethics.org/pub/toughchoices.html.

The faculty case reviewed here is a good example of the individual versus community dilemma and has some elements of a short-term versus long-term dilemma. An example of the truth versus loyalty dilemma might be the Iraqi prisoner abuse case, in which soldiers were faced with reporting abuses by their fellow soldiers (telling the truth) or with being loyal to other members of their unit and remaining quiet. (If you need a refresher on the Abu Ghraib Prison scandal, see www.newyorker.com/fact/content/?040510fa_fact.)

The short-term versus long-term dilemma is one corporate managers face on a regular basis as they try to decide how to balance providing high-dividend returns to investors to maintain their support versus returning some of those profits to research and development and other long-term growth strategies. I'll ask you for an example of the justice versus mercy dilemma in the questions that follow.

Ethics in Organizational Life

It is important to note in this discussion about ethics and leadership that organizations act as both "political arenas" (places in which political activity is going on) and as "political agents" (players in a larger political arena such as an area of business practice, a state system, or an association of organizations.) Our "fractious funding" case study last week was an illustration of organizations as political players. In both of these settings, actors are seeking power and are jockeying with other actors to gain access to and control of scarce resources. Therefore, actors within organizations, and organizations as actors, must always be conscious of the ethical considerations of their activities.

On a personal note, I can't overemphasize the importance of ethical behavior in all of life's activities. What value is there in a life completely focused on self and selfishness? What contribution to the greater good in the world does that life make? If we accept Robert Greenleaf's view from our reading several weeks ago that organizational activity, particularly leadership activity, is (or at least should be) an act of service, then we cannot serve well unless we are always concerned about being ethical. It also has been my observation that when leaders get themselves into trouble, it is generally a reflection of one of three problems: They have ceased to listen, to hear the collective wisdom of those about them; they have been fiscally irresponsible and have not managed finances well; or they have been unethical in some way. Leadership of any kind is often the process of finding the best solutions to ethical dilemmas—many of them the right versus right variety.

If you haven't seen the documentary film, *Enron: The Smartest Guys in the Room*, review the clips that I have included in the Seminar 2 folder or rent the film and watch it by next Wednesday. We have one of our live chat sessions scheduled that day, and I will ask some questions related to the film during that discussion. I highly recommend that you rent and watch the full documentary. It is one of the best case studies I have come across about the abuse of power and of unethical behavior by leaders. It raises questions not only about what is ethical but also about what good leadership means. For this week, give thought to the following questions and post your answers in the forum labeled "Session 2-4: Ethics" on the discussion board. I'm looking forward to your answers!

Question 2-4A:

Cite an example of an activity that might be considered legal but would not be ethical. What is an example of an action that would be ethical but not legal?

Question 2-4B:

Provide an example from your experience of an ethical dilemma that illustrates the choice that sometimes has to be made between mercy and justice.

Question 2-4C:

Read the Hannen and Welch case study in the Seminar 2 folder. What are the ethical issues involved in this case? How would you define those issues in terms of the four dichotomies identified by Kidder?

Project Guidelines

Art History Project

Grading and Deadline

- This project is worth **150 points** and, therefore, is far more important than the final.
- Topic selection is due **September 31.**
- The complete project is due **November 20.**

Learning Objective

What I'd like you to gain from doing this is a deeper knowledge of some particular but important aspect of art that exceeds what most people know. My hope is that because you did this project, someday you will be standing in the Metropolitan Museum in New York, and when you come to a piece that relates to your project topic, you will be able to educate and amaze your friends with your sophisticated understanding of the fine arts.

Project Topic

Select a topic from the list below, and e-mail it to me. If your topic has already been selected by another student (each student must select a different topic), you must choose another (therefore I suggest that you have 2 or 3 options ready). I will write back to you and tell you that your topic is approved or that you need to select an alternative, and I will post a daily list of students/topics so you'll know who has what. Please let me know your topic selection by **September 31.**

List of Topics

Paleolithic cave art

Portrayal of women in Stone Age art

Catal Huyuk

Contrast/compare Paleolithic/Neolithic art

Stonehenge (beyond the scope of the text)

Ancient Sumerian temple construction

Akkadian art and cylinder seals

Stele of Hammurabi

Lion Gate of Mycenae

Khafre

Rosetta Stone

Palette of Narmer

Sphinx (beyond the scope of the text)

Old Kingdom Egyptian temple construction

Middle Kingdom Egyptian temple construction

New Kingdom Egyptian temple construction

Amarna style

Egyptian rock-cut tombs

Depiction of humans in ancient Egyptian art

Cycladic sculpture

Mycenaean architecture

Minoan painting

Portrayal/significance of Athena in Greek art

"Measure of all things" concept and its influence

Greek Geometric period

Greek Orientalizing period

Techniques/significance of Ancient Greek
    pottery

Parthenon

Doric order

Ionic order

Erechtheion

Hellenistic sculpture

Influences behind Etruscan art

Status of women in Etruscan art

Greek influences on Roman art

Pompeii

Roman coins

Construction/significance of the Roman
    Coliseum

Roman illusionism in painting

Roman influences on Christian art

Church of Hagia Sophia

Byzantine churches

Depiction of humans and animals in
    Islamic art

Textiles in the Islamic world

Distinguishing features of Islamic mosques

Characteristics of Early Gothic architecture

Characteristics of High Gothic architecture

Stained glass windows in Gothic art

Cathedral at Chartres

Amiens cathedral

Reims cathedral

Pre-Columbian pyramids in ancient America

Serpent Mound

Early Chinese pagodas

Art during the Tang dynasty

Art during the Han dynasty

Dragon symbolism in Chinese art

Chinese Yangshuo culture

Confucianism in ancient Chinese art

Taoism in ancient Chinese art

Project Parts

Your project must consist of three parts: a written essay (including a bibliography), an artistic presentation, and online discussion.

1. **Essay**

    Body

    - Length: 500 words minimum.
    - Use descriptive language and provide concrete examples to support your ideas. Avoid uninformative sentences like "There were lots of really interesting pyramids constructed in ancient Egypt."
    - When you state facts or discuss ideas that you obtained from another source (whether you quote directly or state in your own words), you must cite the author and date of the source in parentheses in the body of the essay (and list the source in your bibliography).

    Bibliography

    You must use at least 5 resources to research your topic and include these in a bibliography at the end of your essay. Every citation in your essay should correspond to a source listed in the bibliography. Your bibliography may also contain sources you read for background information but did not refer to specifically in the body of your essay. Ideally your bibliography should include a combination of printed publications and Internet resources.

Formatting Examples for Citations and Bibliography

Printed Source:

in text: (Smith, 1990)

bibliography: Smith, J. A. (1990). *The Story of Egyptian Art.* New York: Jones Publishing.

Internet Source:

in text: (Metropolitan Museum, 2004)

bibliography: The Metropolitan Museum of Art. (2004). *Egyptian Art.* Retired June 15, 2006, from www.metmuseum.com.

2. **Artistic Presentation**

- Develop an original artistic (visual) presentation that contributes to, explains, or illustrates some aspect of your topic. You have broad latitude as to how you do this, and creativity is encouraged. For example, you may want to actually produce a piece of art in some particular style we've studied and explain how the technique or subject matter relates to your topic. You can photograph the work and place it in the Unit file. Or you may want to produce a PowerPoint or short video. Just let me know your plans so that we can agree on what's expected.

- You must create your presentation in a format that can be shared online with your classmates. If you do not yet have the computer expertise to do this, please look at the document in the Unit 1 folder titled "How to develop PowerPoint, picture, video, and visual presentations for the Web."

- Presentations must be submitted to me electronically via e-mail. (You may also mail a hard copy to me at [insert address], but I also must have an electronic copy.)

3. **Online Discussion**

During the last month of the class, each of you will lead a brief discussion on the discussion board about your project, describing what you learned and how your artistic presentation contributed to or reflected that learning. I will post your essays and presentations in a special unit file, under Course Content; will create a discussion forum for these discussions; and will notify you at least two weeks in advance of the days on which you need to create your forum and lead your discussion. You will be responsible for making the initial entry for this discussion, so be thinking about what you want to say as you prepare your projects. I'll give further instructions as the dates approach.

Please e-mail me if I can answer any questions.
I'm always happy to help you.
Project Deadline: November 20

Quality Indicators for Community College Online Programs

The 38 quality indicators presented in this appendix were identified through a Delphi Panel conducted by Leo Hirner, director of Distance Learning for the Metropolitan Community College District of Kansas City, as part of a dissertation study. The participants in the study consisted of 15 distance education program leaders in higher education in the Midwest, whose responses were refined through a follow-up survey of stakeholders at four community colleges.

Quality Indicators for Community College Online Programs

Institutional Support

1. The online programs offered by the community college are consistent with the institution's mission and the needs of the community served.

2. The community college supports the online program with the necessary resources to ensure technical infrastructure, training and support personnel, and a full range of faculty and student support services required for online courses and programs.

3. The tuition and fees of online courses and programs are comparable to those paid by on-campus students.

4. A professional, whose primary role is to ensure that academic and student services necessary for student success are in place, oversees the community college online program. The manager fosters collaboration across all institutional services to ensure that online students receive the instructional support, learning resources, and student services necessary for success.

5. The community college's leadership ensures the quality of its online programs by

    a. Promoting the use of best practices for online programs published by regional and national organizations.

    b. Enacting policies and procedures that demonstrate consistency across all forms of instruction.

    c. Demanding that online programs meet the same requirements as on-campus programs.

    d. Pursuing articulation agreements to ensure transfer to regional 4-year colleges and universities.

6. The community college demonstrates its commitment to online programs through support for continued scheduling of online programs to meet the academic needs of students currently enrolled at the institution.

7. A marketing strategy is employed to educate both internal and external constituencies.

    a. Internal marketing takes the form of clear acknowledgment by college leaders of their commitment to the needs of both online and on-campus students, programs and employees, especially the academic equivalence of all offerings.

    b. External marketing activities include

        i. College leadership openly discussing the quality and equivalence of online courses and programs.

        ii. The existence of a comprehensive plan to market online programs that addresses the skills needed for student success and that clearly explains both the academic expectations and time commitment of online courses.

Technical Support

1. The community college provides the necessary infrastructure to ensure connectivity (backbone and bandwidth), storage, redundancy, and system security to meet the needs of current and projected online student populations.
2. A technical support system is in place to meet the needs of students and faculty through a full range of communication options.
3. The community college utilizes a range of information management services that can be integrated to provide smooth access to all technical systems needed to support online programs.
4. A standardized set of Internet tools, including a course management system, has been adopted in support of online courses and programs.
5. Planning for new technology resources for the college includes and integrates online program needs into the budget and execution cycles.
6. Student courseware is available and is consistent from semester to semester.

Curriculum and Instruction

1. The community college supports the development of new online courses through an institutional process with specific development and training benchmarks to be met prior to scheduling.
    a. Development benchmarks should include a department or program peer review to ensure that the online courses meet the same learning outcomes as on-campus courses in the program.
    b. Training benchmarks should include required training in online pedagogy and institutional best practices.
2. The community college provides new online faculty course development support through instructional designers or the training needed to become an instructional designer, and the technical, design, and pedagogical support needed to meet the faculty's instructional goals.
3. A regular schedule of training courses focusing on the technical, pedagogical, and legal rights and responsibilities of online faculty is available to all faculty.
4. The community college supports the philosophy that faculty use each technology for what it does best in meeting the needs of the course or program, emphasizing effective teaching and learning over technology.
5. The college provides faculty sufficient time to develop an online course before it is delivered to students.
6. The institution has a clear policy as to the ownership of the content of its online courses.
7. The college has compiled a set of institutional best practices for online courses and encourages its use by new online faculty during course development. Best practices should include
    a. Response time to student inquiries.
    b. Designing instruction and assessment activities in relation to range of student Internet connectivity.
    c. Timeliness and type of feedback on assignments.
    d. Alternative classroom assessment projects (e.g., discussions or portfolios).

Faculty Support

1. The college encourages faculty participation in professional development addressing online methodology and involvement in peer-to-peer organizations and conferences where issues related to online instruction are examined.
2. Faculty have access to the technology, training, and media resources needed to adequately develop and deliver their online courses.
3. The community college recognizes professionally and rewards faculty for the risk of developing and investing in online education, including course work toward degrees or participation in professional development in accredited online programs.
4. The college supports faculty innovation through pilot projects, alternative scheduling, new innovation, and support for development of alternative teaching methods in compliance with their academic freedom.

Student Support

1. The community college provides preenrollment services to potential students that include access to training about expectations, needed skills (including a prescreening), guidelines, testing policies, program requirements and prerequisites, and technical support available to students taking online classes.
2. The college provides easy-to-find Web-based information geared toward the needs of current online students, including all pertinent information such as schedules, catalogue, policies and procedures, expectations of online courses, FAQs about the online program and common technical problems, explanations of online terminology, and information on available support services.
3. The college provides enrollment procedures that are easy and accessible to online students both online and on ground.
4. An effective, self-directed online orientation is available for new students.
5. Access to traditional on-ground services for online students, including library, career services, and opportunities for professional development and networking are provided to students through a range of communication options not limited to online, on ground, or telephone.
6. The college provides access to learning resource support by
   a. Accommodating online testing by accommodating the range of student Internet connections.
   b. Providing access to on-site and off-site proctored testing options.
   c. Training lab and library personnel in support of online student needs.
   d. Providing online access to library collections and electronic reserves through institutional resources or in conjunction with regional partnerships.
7. Student academic honor and service programs give equal consideration to both online and traditional course work and activities.

Evaluation and Assessment

1. Regular evaluations of online courses and the learning support infrastructure, consistent with that used for other courses, are required by the community college.
2. Online faculty evaluations account for online delivery, instructional methods, and practices.

3. Program evaluations are used to improve programs; aid in institutional decision-making; assess stakeholders' access to technology, the range of services provided, and course offerings; and address barriers and challenges to online instruction. These evaluations serve to provide program outcomes for funding agencies.

4. Online students and faculty are regularly surveyed about the range of services, policies supporting online programs, and their satisfaction with the online experience.

5. Faculty receive regular and objective feedback from students about their courses and instruction.

6. The college utilizes assessment methods recommended by accrediting agencies for distance courses (e.g. Council for Higher Education Accreditation or North Central Association); including student persistence and attrition in online classes and assessment of student learning outcomes in online courses as compared to traditional modes of instruction.

7. Online assessment and evaluation tools are designed to ensure the anonymity of respondents.

Note. Adapted from Hirner (2006) by permission.

Index

A

abbreviations in e-mails, avoiding, 56

academic administrators
class size issues, 35
faculty recruitment issues, 33
in loco parentis doctrine, 80
online teaching as limbo, 32
See also administrative support

academic dishonesty, 3, 85, 87–88, 91–95

academic malpractice, 32

academic support. *See* student support

accessibility issues
aptitude for online teaching, 30–33
and copyright, 99, 101
disabled students, 69, 101, 102–103
distance education history, 5, 9
distance education today, 14
and early contact, 20
facilitating discussion, 57–58
legal considerations, 102–103
and student success, 22
and student work commitments, 17

achievement, student, 8, 80

Achieving the Dream: Community Colleges
Count initiative, 16

active learning strategies, 45, 51–61
See also collaborative learning

Active Reviewing Guide, 76

adjunct instructors, 9–10, 33

administrative support, 19–20
See also academic administrators

Adobe software, 68, 69

adult education
distance education history, 5
facilitating discussion, 55
incorporating learning principles, 45–46
lecture as learning catalyst, 46–47

African American students, 15

age (of students)
distance education today, 15
incorporating learning principles, 45–46
lecture as learning catalyst, 46–47
in loco parentis doctrine, 79
and student orientations, 26

agendas
course management basics, 2, 43–44, 49
facilitating discussion, 55
samples, 39–40, 43–44, 134–136

AIFF files, 69

Air Force Survival School, 27

American Council on Education, 12

Americans with Disabilities Act, 102, 103

andragogy, research on, 45–46

animation, Web, 65

Annenburg Foundation, 8

announcements
as asynchronous communication, 9
and audiovisual tools, 69
creating and using, 41–43
repetition benefits, 43
sample, *42*
student announcements page, 73
student characteristics, 20
and syllabus development, 38

Apple QuickTime, 71

applied discussion, increased use of, 46–47

archiving and activation tools, 51

Arem, Cynthia, 22

argumentative discussion, 29–30

    See also discussion *entries*

Armstrong (2000), 12

art history course example

    announcement, 42

    facilitating discussion, 53–54

    graphic enhancements, *66, 67*

    sample project guidelines, 48, 141–143

    scheduling issues, 109

Art Instruction Schools, 7

artists' rights, 98

    See also copyright issues

assessment. *See* course assessment and

    evaluation; self-assessment *entries;*

    student assessment

Assignment Manager tool, 48–50

assignments

    academic dishonesty issues, 3, 85, 87–88, 91–95

    building community through, 47–48

    grade book creation, 48–49

    privacy issues, 104

    sample project guidelines, 48, 141–143

    tools for posting, 49

    See also specific aspects

Assignments menu item, 43

Assistive Technology Act, 103

asynchronous communication, examples of, 9, 14

    See also specific types

at-risk students

    biography examples, 19

    in local parentis ideals, 84

    minimizing risk, 18–19

    risk factors, 16–17

    and student orientations, 26

attachments to e-mails. *See* e-mail attachments

attendance, and millennials, 21

audio files, Sun, 69

audiotapes of lectures, 47

audio tracks, 68–69, 71

audiovisual technology

    distance education future, 111

    distance education history, 7–8

tools overview, 3, 63–73

    See also video *entries; specific technologies*

Audition, Adobe, 69

authors' rights, 98, 102

    See also copyright issues

autonomous learners, adults as, 45

AVI files, 71

B

background noise in recordings, 69

Baldwin-Wallace College, 108

Bangura (2003), 45

Berne copyright convention, 100

bibliographic citations, 87, 98

biographies, student. *See* student biographies

Blackboard

    acquisition of WebCT, 75

    course management basics, 41, 43, 48–50

    platform overviews, 75

    sample instructions, 131–133

Blackstone, William, 79

Bloom, Benjamin, 57

bookstores, 37

brainstorming, 59

Buckley Amendment, 103–104

budget issues. *See* financial issues

bulletins, 9

Burns, Jim, 31, 34

C

cable television, 9, 11

calendars, 2, 43–44, 49

    See also agendas

Calvert Day School, 7

cameras, 11, 60, 68, 72

campus bookstore, 37

Campus Computing Project, 11–12

campus culture, student inclusion in, 79, 80

Campus Pipeline, 75

Carlson (2005), 21–22, 33

Carnegie Commission on Higher Education, 8

Carnwell's categories of support, 19–20

Carriuolo (2002), 12, 13

case studies, increased use of, 46–47

CDs, 37, 71

cells, in Web animation, 65

certification, granting of, 111

charts, quick reference, *81*, 83

chat sessions

    and collaborative learning, 59–60

    course management basics, 47, 48, 50–51

Chautauqua Institute, 6

cheating. *See* academic dishonesty

Chickering and Gamson (1987), 45, 57

citations, bibliographic, 87, 98

class directories, 68

class discussion. *See* discussion *entries*

class excursions, 72–73

classroom space issues, 106, 110

class rosters, 36, 104

class size

    course management basics, 50–51

    facilitating discussion, 57

    online course issues, 35–36

    and student assessment, 90

clipart, 64–65

cognitive processing, levels of, 57

Cohen and Brawer (2003), 15

collaborative learning

    academic dishonesty issues, 95

    assignment examples, 48

    building personal connections, 84

    critics of online learning, 12

    and faculty orientations, 34

    hybrid courses, 106, 107

    and millennials, 22

    strategies for, 3, 58–61

    and synchronous tools, 50–51

    terminology, 58

    and webcams, 72

    See also learning communities; small groups

collaborative teaching partnerships, 111

college laboratories, 37

College of DuPage, 25

college ownership of copyrights, 102

college publications, and slander, 104

The Colliery Engineer School of Mines, 7

Collison et al. (2000), 19, 29–30

color resolution, 68

Columbia Basin College, 26–27

commercial value and copyrights, 99, 100

Common Cartridge, 75, 77

community colleges

    copyright ownership, 102

    distance education history, 5, 9–10

    distance education today, 2, 13

    institutional support, 146

    online learning research for, 19–20

Community College Survey of Student

    Engagement, 12

compression of files, 65, 68–70

computer-generated course work. *See*

    Web-based instruction

computer hardware

    and audiovisual technology, 71

    course management basics, 47

    and precourse letter, 37

    and student orientations, 23–24, 26, 27

    and techno-whiz instructors, 33

    See also specific types

computer literacy. *See* technological literacy

computer projectors, 14, 32

computer servers for video, 71

computer software

    and audiovisual technology, 71

    course management basics, 47

    for photo editing, 68

    and precourse letter, 37

    and student orientations, 23–24, 27

    for Web animations, 65

    See also specific types

computer use statistics, 11

confidentiality issues. *See* privacy issues

contracts, and copyright, 102

Control Panel menu item, 41–42, 48

Convene ac@deme, 75

cooperative learning. *See* collaborative learning

co-ops, teaching, 111

copying work of other students, 85, 88, 92–95

    See also academic dishonesty

Copyright Act, 99–101

copyright issues

academic dishonesty, 3, 85, 87–88

"All Rights Reserved" use, 100

fair use, 3, 98–101

materials protected by, 97–98, 100

Moodle platform, 78

myths about, 100–101

and online instructors, 101

ownership for students and faculty, 102

performance rights, 101

photograph use, 68

video use, 71

Cornell University, 6, 7

corporal punishment, 79

Corporation for Public Broadcasting, 8

correspondence, e-mail. *See* e-mail *entries*

correspondence courses

distance education history, 5–7

distance education today, 11

Correspondence School of Hebrew, 6

cost issues. *See* financial issues

course archiving and activation tools, 51

course assessment and evaluation, 38, 148–149

course content, and course management, 41

Course Content menu item, 43, 47, 48

course design, 37–38, 45

See also specific aspects

course development providers, 76

Course Documents menu item, 43, 47, 48

course evaluation and assessment, 38, 148–149

course export and import tools, 51

course groundwork, 2, 20, 35–40

See also specific aspects

Course Information menu item, 43, 56

course loads (student), 19

course management

basics of, 2–3, 41–51

student support needs, 20

See also specific aspects

course management platforms

course management basics, 41–43, 48–50

overview of, 3, 75–78

and student orientations, 23, 26, 27

See also Blackboard; WebCT

course management systems

course management basics, 41–43, 48–51

and faculty orientations, 34

and hybrid courses, 106–107

open-source system reviews, 3, 76–78

platform overviews, 3, 75–78

and student orientations, 23

and test proctoring, 88–89

See also specific systems

Course Map menu item, 41

course materials

collaborative exercises, 58

copyright issues, 3, 68, 71, 97–102

course development providers, 76

facilitating discussion, 55

lecture as learning catalyst, 47

open-source materials, 111

and precourse letter, 37

samples, 4, 123–143

See also specific types

course objectives, and course design, 37–38, 39

course prerequisites, 23, 25

course size. *See* class size

course structure, student support needs, 20, 38–39

course subdivisions, 2, 38–39, 111

See also seminars

court system, 79, 100, 104

See also legal issues

credentialing, universal, 112

credit lines, 98

criminal copyright violations, 101

Cross (1999), 17, 46

Crowder College, 24–25, 112–113

current state of distance education, 1, 2, 11–14

curriculum and instruction quality indicators, 147

Curtin University of Technology, 77

D

Darwin, Charles, 39

debates, as collaborative learning, 59

degrees, granting of, 111–112

derivative works, 99, 101

See also copyright issues

developmental students, 16, 17, 46

dialogue. *See* discussion *entries*

digital cameras, 68

   See also webcams

digital drop box, 48

digital technology

   copyright issues, 99, 101

   distance education history, 9

   See also audiovisual technology; Web *entries*

Diploma Correspondence College, 7

directories, class, 68

directory information privacy, 103

disabilities

   aptitude for online teaching, 33

   and audio tracks, 69

   and copyright, 101

   federal laws relating to, 102–103

disciplinary issues, 79, 95

   See also academic dishonesty

discussion, facilitating

   aptitude for online teaching, 29–32, 34

   lecture as learning catalyst, 46–47

   strategies for, 3, 53–58

   student support needs, 20, 38–39

   See also student participation

discussion, threaded. *See* threaded discussion

discussion boards

   as asynchronous communication, 9

   at-risk students, 18–19

   building personal connections, 83

   and collaborative learning, 59–60

   course management basics, 47, 50–51

   distance education today, 14

   encouraging individual work, 88

   facilitating discussion, 53–58

   and hybrid courses, 106, 107

   student social forums, 56, 73

discussion questions, framing, 56–58

dishonesty, academic, 3, 85, 87–88, 91–95

display settings, 68

distance education

   current state of, 1, 2, 11–14

   future of, 4, 111–113

   history of, 1, 2, 5–10

   terminology, 7, 12

   See also Web-based instruction; *specific aspects*

distributed education, terminology, 12

documents, posting and exchanging, 48–49

Dougiamas, Martin, 77

download time issues. *See* Internet connections

Draves, William, 39

Durham Technical College, 105

DVDs, 37, 71

dyads, 48

   See also collaborative learning; small groups

E

Earthcam.com, 72

East Central Community College, 78

eCollege.com, 75

Edison, Thomas, 7–8

educational backgrounds of students, 15

educational rights, 103–104

   See also legal issues; *specific aspects*

e-Education, 75

effectiveness, faculty. *See* faculty effectiveness

eLearning orientation, 26–27

electronically hybridized courses. *See* hybrid courses

Elluminate, 63

e-mail attachments

   aptitude for online teaching, 31

   document exchange basics, 48–49

   privacy issues, 104

   student orientations, 24

e-mails

   abbreviations in, 56

   and academic dishonesty, 92–95

   as asynchronous communication, 9

   course management basics, 43, 48–49, 51

   faculty accessibility issues, 22, 30, 31

   and hybrid courses, 106

   and precourse letters, 36, 37

   privacy issues, 104

   security issues, 24, 49

   slang and jargon in, 56

   and student orientations, 24, 25

   and student profiles, 19

   and student responsibility, 85

   timely response to, 20

e-mail systems

privacy issues, 104
    student orientations, 23, 24
emotional support, 19–20
    See also student support
English common law, 79, 99
English composition courses
    class size, 35, 90
    scheduling, 109
English skills
    and academic dishonesty, 92–95
    developmental assistance needs, 16, 17
    See also writing skills
enhanced graphics, 63–67
enrollments
    and at-risk students, 17
    and class size, 35
    distance education history, 9
    diversity and collaboration, 58
    and millennials, 21–22
    and rosters, 36
entertainment industry, and copyright, 101
equal access. *See* accessibility issues
Erben, Tony, 60
ethical issues
    academic dishonesty, 3, 85, 87–88, 91–95
    and Internet radicals, 97
ethics lecture example
    facilitating discussion, 54–55, 57
    sample discussion and questions, 47, 137–140
Europe, distance education history, 6, 7, 9
    See also specific institutions
evaluations. *See* course assessment and
    evaluation; faculty evaluation
examples, increased use of, 46–47
exams
    and academic dishonesty, 88–90
    and hybrid courses, 107
    privacy issues, 103–104
exchanging and posting documents, 48–49
excursions for classes, 72–73
expulsion, and academic dishonesty, 95

F

face-to-face meetings, 83–84, 105–108

facilitating discussion. *See* discussion, facilitating
faculty accessibility. *See* accessibility issues
faculty as mentors, 12, 46
faculty characteristics
    aptitude for online teaching, 2, 14, 29–34
    distance education future, 111–113
    distance education today, 14
    facilitating discussion, 56
    and open-source providers, 78
faculty contact with students. *See* personal contact
    with students; *specific aspects*
faculty control panel, 41–42, 48
faculty co-ops, 111
faculty course management. *See* course management
faculty development. *See* faculty orientations;
    faculty training
faculty effectiveness
    aptitude for online teaching, 2, 14, 29, 32–34
    distance education today, 12–13, 14
faculty evaluation
    quality indicators, 148–149
    remote staff as challenge, 33
faculty intellectual property rights, 102
faculty irresponsibility, 32
faculty load, 35–36
faculty orientations
    and academic dishonesty, 92
    and course management tools, 51
    elements of, 33–34
    and self-assessment, 32
faculty parental role, 79–85
faculty participation in discussions
    aptitude for online teaching, 29, 30
    facilitating discussion, 55–58
    personal contact strategies, 20
faculty recruitment, 33
faculty support, quality indicators, 148
faculty support groups, 34
faculty time management. *See* time management
faculty training
    aptitude for online teaching, 31, 32
    audiovisual tools overview, 3, 63–73
    distance education history, 9–10
    and faculty support groups, 34

and hybrid courses, 106
in loco parentis ideals, 80
remote staff as challenge, 33
fair use, 3, 98–101
familiarity with students
at-risk students, 18–19
in loco parentis ideals, 83–85
overfamiliarity as issue, 22
See also personal contact with students;
student biographies
Family Educational Rights and Privacy Act, 103–104
The Federal Schools, 7
feedback
as online teaching challenge, 32, 80–81
and student responsibility, 85
See also grades; specific aspects
films, instructional, 7–8
See also video entries
filtering of e-mails, 24, 49
financial aid needs, as risk factor, 16
financial issues
class size considerations, 35
distance education today, 5, 14
open-source learning systems, 3, 76–78
value and copyrights, 99, 100
Fireworks, Macromedia, 65
First Amendment, and copyright, 98
first sale doctrine, 101
Flash, Macromedia, 65
folders, unit or seminar
course groundwork basics, 39
course management basics, 43, 47, 48
font selection, 64
Foothill-De Anza Community College District, 76
foreign language classes, paired practice for, 60, 72
forums for discussion. See discussion boards
Foster, Thomas J., 7
frames, in Web animation, 65
framing questions, 56–58
free course management systems, 3, 76–78

G

games, interactive, 60–61, 76
Gehring (2000), 45, 46

GIF format, 65, 68
good practice indicators, 45, 57
See also quality issues
Google, for detecting plagiarism, 88
grades
and academic dishonesty, 92–95
collaborative exercises, 59, 60
facilitating discussion, 56, 57
grade book creation, 49–50
privacy issues, 103–104
graphics
in animation, 65
copyright protection for, 97, 100
enhanced, 63–67
See also photographs
Group functions, 51
group learning. See collaborative learning
group presentations and panels, 60, 107
group size, 48, 50–51
See also small groups

H

hardware. See computer hardware
Harper, William Rainey, 6, 7
hearing impairments, 33
Hermod, Hans S., 7
high-color settings, 68
Hill, Marty, 43
Hill, Patrick, 108–109
Hirner, Leo, 145
history of distance education, 1, 2, 5–10
Hotmail, 24, 104
Hot Potatoes, 76
HTML (Hypertext Markup Language), 71–72
hybrid courses
distance education today, 11–12
and learning communities, 110
overview of, 3–4, 105–108

I

icebreakers, introductory, 18
icons, 41, 98
Illinois Online Network, 24, 63
illustrated documents, creating, 48

images. *See* graphics; photographs

Indiana University, 76

individualized group learning, online education as, 17

Individuals with Disabilities Education Act, 103

individual work, encouraging, 84–85

    See also academic dishonesty

in loco parentis ideals, 79–85

Instant Web Audio, 69

institutional support, quality indicators, 146

instructional films, 7–8

instructional radio, 8

instructional television

    distance education history, 8–9

    distance education today, 11

Instructional Television Fixed Service, 9

instructors. *See* faculty *entries*

intellectual development of students, 17, 64

intellectual property issues, 97, 102

    See also copyright issues

interaction types, 20

interactive games, 60–61, 76

International Correspondence Schools, 7

International Data Corporation, 11

Internet

    and academic dishonesty, 87–88

    and disability laws, 103

    distance education history, 9

    distance education today, 11, 14

    and HTML, 71

    Net generation students, 21–22, 33

    See also Web *entries;* World Wide Web

Internet connections

    and audiovisual tools, 65, 69–71

    and precourse letters, 37

    and student orientations, 23–24

Internet resources. *See* Web resources

Internet security, 24, 49, 104

introductory letters. *See* precourse letters

irresponsible faculty members, 32

isolation issues, 20, 81, 83, 84

    See also psychological distance as issue

item analysis for tests, 89

IT staff

computer servers for video, 71

course management tools, 51

and hybrid courses, 106

orientation development, 26

See also technical support

J

jargon, avoiding, 56

Jeopardy templates, 61, 76

Joint Council on Educational Television, 8

JPEG format, 68

judicial system, 79, 100, 104

    See also legal issues

K

Kemp (2002), 17, 20

King, Millie, academic dishonesty case study, 91–95

Klos, Karen, 78

Knowles, Malcomb, 45

L

Langan, Terri, 89–90, 106

Langenscheidt, Gustav, 6

language classes, paired practice for, 60, 72

Lapore and Wilson (1958), 8

learner interaction types, 20

learning communities

    at-risk students, 19

    building, 4, 47–48, 105, 108–110

    described, 108–109

    and hybrid courses, 106

    and pragmatic dialogue, 30

    and precourse letters, 37

    and student characteristics, 22

learning disabilities. *See* disabilities

learning games, 60–61, 76

learning guides, and student orientations, 25–26

learning objectives, 37–38, 39

learning outcomes, 13, 108

learning principles, incorporating, 44–46, 48

learning units. *See* course subdivisions; seminars

lectures

    and hybrid courses, 106–107

    as learning catalyst, 46–47

See also ethics lecture example

Lederman (2006), 75

legal issues

    accessibility for disabled, 101, 102–103

    educational rights, 103–104

    ethics lecture example, 54–55

    in loco parentis doctrine, 79–85

    slander, 104

    See also copyright issues

letters, introductory. *See* precourse letters

LexisNexis Statistical Web site, 11

libraries

    copyright issues, 101

    distance education today, 14

    and precourse letters, 37

    test proctoring, 89

Lindeman, Michael W., 63

links, and HTML, 72

log in instructions, 36

logos, 98

looping animations, 68

Lumina Foundation, 16

Luzar, Elizabeth, 89

M

Macintosh format, 26, 69

Macromedia software, 65

malpractice, academic, 32

manuals for course management systems, 51

maps, of student locations, 83

Martyn, Margie, 108

Massachusetts Institute of Technology, 76

mathematics skills, developmental assistance needs, 16

McClelland's theory of student involvement, 80

meaning, conveying, 14, 30

    See also writing skills

meeting in person, 83–84, 105–108

Mellon Foundation, 76

mentoring, 12, 46

menu bars

    audiovisual tools overview, 75

    course management basics, 41–43, 47, 50–51

    student orientation example, 26

See also Blackboard; WebCT

message boards for students, 73

Meyer (2002), 13

microphones, Web, 60

microwave technology, 8–9

MIDI files, 69

millennials

    aptitude for online teaching, 33

    lecture as learning catalyst, 47

    student characteristics, 21–22

minority students, 15

MIT, 76

modularized approach. *See* course subdivisions; seminars

Moodle, 3, 77–78

Moody Correspondence School, 7

Moore (1989), 20, 38

moral rights, 98

    See also copyright issues

Mortensen, Ernst G., 7

Mountain Empire Community College, 16

movie frame rates, 68

Movie Picture Experts Group (MPEG) files, 71

multimedia technology. *See* audiovisual technology

multiple-choice assessments, 89

multitasking by students, 21

Muse (2004), 26

Musical Instrument Digital Interface files, 69

music files, 69, 100

N

Napster, 100

National Center for Educational Statistics, 16–17

Native American students, 15

Net generation students, 21–22, 33

    See also millennials

netiquette, 56

Network Teacher Enhancement Coalition, 29

Norsk Korrespondanseskole, 7

O

office hours, 12, 31

online booksellers, 37

online delivery systems. *See* course management

systems

online instruction. *See* Web-based instruction

online orientations. *See* faculty orientations; student orientations

online research paper catalogs, 88

online resources. *See* Web resources

Online Writing Lab, 76

open-book assignments, 90

OpenCourseWare, 76

open-ended dialogue, allowing for, 56

open-source course management systems, 3, 76–78

open-source course materials, 111

Open University, 9

orientations. *See* faculty orientations; student orientations

Osborne (2001), 26

outcomes, learning, 13, 108

overfamiliarity as issue, 22

owners of copyright. *See* copyright issues

P

paint applications, 68

Paint Shop Pro, 68

paired practice, 60, 72

panels, and collaborative learning, 60

Parade of Games, 76

parental capacity, acting in, 79–85

parental rights, 103–104

part-time students, 15–19

 See also work commitments of students

Patrick Henry Community College, 19

pedagogical principles, 44–46, 77–78

peer reviews by students, 59

Pennsylvania State College, 7

performance rights, 101

permissions

 and copyright ownership, 98

 for derivative works, 101

 and fair use, 99, 100, 101

 for photograph use, 68

 for video use, 71

 See also copyright issues

Perry's intellectual development stages, 17

personal contact with students

in loco parentis ideals, 79–85

 overfamiliarity as issue, 22

 strategies for, 20–21

 See also familiarity with students; *specific aspects*

personal skills inventory. *See* self-assessment *entries*

Phillipps, Caleb, 2, 5–6

photographs

 audiovisual tools overview, 65, 68, 71, 73

 building personal connections, 83

 copyright protection for, 97

 See also graphics

Photoshop, Adobe, 68

physical sciences course example, 112–113

pictures. *See* graphics; photographs

piracy, Web, 98

 See also copyright issues

Pitman, Sir Isaac, 6

pixel count, 68

plagiarism, 3, 85, 87–88, 92–95

 See also copyright issues

players

 for audio files, 69

 for DVDs, 37

plug-ins, 65, 69, 71

point-based grading

 collaborative exercises, 59

 creating grade books, 50

 facilitating discussion, 56

 See also grades

posting and exchanging documents, 48–49

PowerPoint

 audiovisual tools overview, 65

 document exchange basics, 49

 game templates, 76

 and hybrid courses, 107

 for online lectures, 47

 for student orientations, 27

pragmatic dialogue, 29–30

 See also discussion *entries*

precourse letters

 elements of, 20, 36–37

 sample, 36, 37, 124–125

 and syllabus development, 38

prerequisites, 23, 25

presentations by groups, 60, 107

privacy issues

with e-mail, 49

and FERPA, 3, 103–104

private group exchanges, 51

proctors, 88–89

professional development. *See* faculty orientations;

faculty training

profiles, student. *See* student biographies

projectors, computer, 14, 32

psychological distance as issue

aptitude for online teaching, 32

course groundwork, 38

student characteristics, 20, 22

See also isolation issues

Public Broadcasting System, 8

public domain materials, 97–99

See also copyright issues; open-source *entries*

publishing industry, and copyright, 99, 101

Purdue University, 76

Q

quality issues

distance education today, 13, 14

facilitating discussion, 57

good practice indicators, 45, 57

online programs quality indicators, 145–149

personal contact with instructors, 79

question formulation, 56–58, 88

question pools for tests, 89

quick reference charts, *81*, 83

QuickTime, Apple, 71

quizzes, and academic dishonesty, 89

R

radio, instructional, 8

ram, video, 68

reading skills, developmental assistance needs, 16, 17

See also English skills

RealAudio, 69

real time communication. *See* synchronous communication

RealVideo, 71

recordings, audio and video. *See* audio and

video *entries*

recruitment, of faculty, 33

redundancy, usefulness of, 43

reference lists and citations, 87, 98

registration, 23, 36

Rehabilitation Act, 102–103

repetition, usefulness of, 43

research design and methodology issues, 13

research paper catalogs, online, 88

resiliency skills of students, 17

resources

aptitude for online teaching, 32

course design issues, 37–38

directing students to, 20–21

distance education today, 14

See also Course materials; Web resources

retirees

collaborative partnerships, 111

finding online faculty, 33

as proctors, 89

Reviewing Guide, Active, 76

reviews, peer, 59

risk factors for students, 16–17, 19

See also at-risk students

Robinson, Jackie, 39

role playing, 60

rosters, 36, 104

rural areas

distance education history, 7

distance education today, 13–14

diversity and collaboration, 58

Russell (1999), 13

Rustinches Fernlehrinstitut, 7

S

Saba (1988), 20, 38

Sakai, 3, 76–77

satellite technology, 8–9

Sauk Valley Community College, 25–26

scanning photographs, 68

Scavenger Hunt templates, 76

Schade, Herb, 112–113

scheduling

and co-ops, 111

and hybrid courses, 105–107
and learning communities, 109–110
See also agendas; calendars; office hours
Schreck, Jane, 35, 87
security, Internet, 24, 49, 104
self-assessment (of faculty)
aptitude for online teaching, 29–33
checklist for, *31*
course design issues, 38
self-assessment (of students)
and student orientations, 25
seminars
course management basics, 43, 44, 47, 48
and student support needs, 38–39
using, 39–40
See also course subdivisions
Shaked, Edith, 39
Shea, Virginia, 56
sidebar forums, 56, 73
Sinclair Community College, 27
single parents
distance education today, 13–14
student characteristics, 18, 19
students at risk, 16
size of classes. *See* class size
slanderous content, 104
slang, avoiding, 56
slide shows, 68
small groups
building personal connections, 84
collaborative exercise strategies, 58–59, 60
course management basics, 48, 50–51
facilitating discussion, 57
See also collaborative learning
Smart Boards, 14, 32–33
social discussion, aptitude for online teaching, 29–30
See also discussion *entries*
social forums for students, 56, 73
socialization
at-risk students, 18–19
distance education today, 12, 13
social security numbers, 103–104
The Society to Encourage Study at Home, 6
socioeconomic characteristics of students, 15

Sofia program, 76
software. *See* computer software
sound files, 69
See also audio *entries*
Southwest Technical College, 25
spam control, 49
Spanier, Graham, 105
specialists, as class resource, 48
speech courses, 14
speech impairments, 33
speech recordings, 47, 68–69
Stanford University, 76
State University of Iowa, 8
statistical functions of grade books, 50
streaming audio, 69
streaming video, 48, 69, 70–71, 72
structured learning
and audiovisual tools, 64
incorporating learning principles, 46
and millennials, 22
and underprepared students, 17
student achievement, 8, 80
student ages. *See* age (of students)
student announcements page, 73
student assessment
and hybrid courses, 107
online world complexities, 92
privacy issues, 103–104
and student orientations, 23, 25, 27
techniques overview, 3, 89–91
See also grades
student biographies
at-risk students, 18–19
photograph use, 73, *81*, 83
and student orientations, 23
student characteristics
distance education today, 14
review of, 1, 2, 15–22
and student orientations, 25, 26
See also specific aspects
student contact. *See* personal contact with students
student course loads, 19
student dishonesty, 3, 85, 87–88, 91–95
student engagement

and audiovisual tools, 64

and course management tools, 51

distance education today, 12–13

and psychological distance, 20

See also student involvement; student participation

student information, quick reference charts, *81, 83*

See also student biographies; student records

student intellectual property rights, 102

student involvement

in local parentis ideals, 79–85

Tinto's theory of, 80

See also student engagement; student participation

student motivation, biography examples, 19

student names, faculty use of, 20–21

student orientations

advantages of, 2, 23, 28

and audiovisual tools, 69

and course groundwork, 35–37

development of, 26–27

elements of, 23–24

examples of, 24–26

and faculty support groups, 34

removing the fear, 27–28

student participation

in class excursions, 73

in collaborative exercises, 58–59

distance education today, 12, 14

facilitating discussion, 53–58

and faculty availability, 31

fostering responsibility, 85

and webcams, 72

See also student engagement; student involvement

student peer reviews, 59

student persistence, 13, 19

student photographs, 68, 73, 83

student records

privacy issues, 103–104

quick reference charts, *81, 83*

student responsibility

fostering, 84–85

and learning communities, 109–110

See also academic dishonesty

student rights, 102, 103–104

See also legal issues; *specific aspects*

student rosters, 36, 104

student satisfaction

distance education today, 13

in local parentis ideals, 80, 84

and roster provision, 36

student social forums, 56, 73

student support

course groundwork, 38–39

critics of online learning, 12

distance learning requirements, 19–20

and hybrid courses, 4

and learning communities, 108

quality indicators, 148

requirements for online learning, 19–20

student-to-student interaction, 84, 105

See also collaborative learning; small groups

study materials. *See* course materials

Sun audio files, 69

survival school orientation approach, 27–28

Sweeney, Richard T., 21–22

syllabus

and academic dishonesty, 88, 94, 95

course management basics, 43, 50

facilitating discussion, 55

and graphic enhancement, *66, 67*

preparing and using, 2, 37–38

repetition benefits, 43

sample, 38, 126–130

student characteristics, 20, 21

synchronized audio, 68

synchronous communication

aptitude for online teaching, 34

audiovisual tools overview, 72

building personal connections, 84

course management basics, 48, 50–51

examples of, 9

and hybrid courses, 108

See also specific types

synthesizers, music, 69

system administrators. *See* IT staff

T

teachers. *See* faculty *entries*

technical support

quality indicators, 147
and student orientations, 26
See also IT staff
technological literacy
aptitude for online teaching, 30–33
audiovisual tools overview, 3, 63–73
and course management tools, 51, 78
distance education today, 12, 14
and faculty orientations, 34
and netiquette, 56
and student characteristics, 21–22
and student orientations, 24–26, 26, 28
Telecommunications Act, 103
teleconferencing, 5, 8
telecourses, 11
television, instructional, 8–9, 11
Telstar I satellite, 8
term of protection for copyright, 98, 101
tests
and academic dishonesty, 88–90
and hybrid courses, 107
privacy issues, 103–104
textbooks, 37, 46–47, 102
textual information, and audiovisual tools, 63–65
Think–Pair–Share technique, 60
threaded discussion
aptitude for online teaching, 32
and at-risk students, 18–19
building personal connections, 83
and hybrid courses, 107
strategies for, 53–56
See also discussion *entries*
Ticknor, Anna Eliot, 6
time issues with downloads. *See* Internet connections
timelines for discussion postings, 56
See also agendas; calendars
timely response to e-mails, 20
time management
course management basics, 2–3, 41–51
and hybrid courses, 3–4, 105–107
and learning communities, 109–110
and student assessment, 90
and student orientations, 23, 28, 35
timing of tests, 89

Tinto's theory of departure, 80
Toussaint, Charles, 6
Trivia templates, 76

U

underprepared students, 17, 25
United States, distance education history, 5–9
See also specific institutions
Universal Credentialing Standard, 112
University of Chicago, 6, 7
University of Illinois, 24, 63
University of London, 6
University of Michigan, 76
University of Texas, 99
University of the Air, 9
University of Wisconsin, 6–7, 7
urban areas, diversity and collaboration, 58
U.S. Congress, 101
U.S. Constitution, and copyright, 98, 99
U.S. Copyright Office, 101
U.S. Department of Education, 103
U.S. Federal Communications Commission, 8, 9
U.S. history class example, 60
U.S. laws. *See* legal issues

V

Van Hise, Charles, 7
Van Rensselaer, Martha, 7
video clips, 37, 48, 65, 69–71
See also films, instructional
video conferencing
distance education history, 5, 8
video ram, 68
videotapes of lectures, 47
Virtual Classroom features, 50–51, 59–60
viruses, computer, 24
See also Internet security
vision impairments, 69, 101
visual technology. *See* audiovisual technology; video *entries*

W

water cooler forums, 56, 73
wave files, 69

Web animation, 65
Web-based instruction
    advantages of, 1, 2, 12–14
    audiovisual tools overview, 3, 63–73
    class size issues, 35–36
    critics of, 1, 12
    and disability laws, 103
    distance education history, 2, 5
    distance education today, 2, 11–14
    future of, 4, 111–113
    as instructional limbo, 32
    research on community colleges, 19–20
    terminology, 9
    Web resources for, *37*
    See also specific aspects
Web browser plug-ins, 65, 69, 71
webcams, 11, 60, 72, 105–106
WebCT
    acquisition by Blackboard, 75
    course management basics, 41, 42
    platform overviews, 75
    and student orientations, 25–26
Web microphones, 60
Web page menus. *See* menu bars
Web piracy, 98
    See also copyright issues
Web resources
    and academic dishonesty, 87–88, *93*
    assessing Internet content, *100*
    for audiovisual tools, 63, 69, *70*
    for collaborative exercises, 58, 61
    copyright issues, 97–102
    for course development, 76–78
    for course management, 3, 47, 48, *77*
    distance education today, 14
    and hybrid courses, 107
    for online orientations, *24*
    for online teaching, *37*
    and seminar use, 39–40
    See also resources
Web searches, using, 48, 88, 107
Wesleyan University, 6

Western Governor's University, 111
Wheeler (2002), 19, 20, 38
Whiteboard and Chat features, 50–51
Windows format, 25, 69
wireless networks, 11–12
Wolsey Hall, 7
women as students
    and audio tracks, 69
    distance education history, 7
    distance education today, 13–14
    student characteristics, 15
work commitments of students
    and audio tracks, 69
    student characteristics, 15, 17, 18–19
    and student orientations, 26
    students at risk, 16, 17
works for hire, 102
world religions course example
    agenda, 43–44, 134–136
    brainstorming technique, 59
    precourse letter, 36, 37, 124–125
    scheduling issues, 109
    student assessment, 90
    syllabus, 38, 126–130
    Web resources, 14, 48
World War II, distance education history, 8
World Wide Web
    distance education future, 112
    distance education history, 9
    and HTML, 71
    See also Internet *entries;* Web *entries*
writing skills
    and academic dishonesty, 87, 93
    aptitude for online teaching, 14, 30, 32, 33
    and faculty orientations, 34
    framing questions, 56–58
    Online Writing Lab, 76
    student characteristics, 18
    and student orientations, 25
    and student responsibility, 85
    See also English skills

About the Authors

Kent Farnsworth is Mary Ann Lee Endowed Professor in the Community College Leadership Academy at the University of Missouri–St. Louis (UMSL) and director of the Center for International Community College Education and Leadership. Before accepting the directorship of the UMSL Academy, he served as president of Crowder College in Neosho, Missouri, for 19 years. He has more than 30 years of experience in higher education administration, including service as dean of students with the Eastern Iowa Community College District and director of admissions at Missouri's Truman State University. Before entering the education profession, he worked in production management for National Semiconductor Corporation in Santa Clara, California, and spent 5 years as a pilot in the U.S. Air Force. In addition to his directorship at the university, Farnsworth teaches courses in community college administration and leadership in the College of Education.

His academic background represents a diverse blend of both public and private education, beginning with high school years spent in a parochial school in Tehran, Iran. Farnsworth holds a bachelor's degree in political science from Brigham Young University, master's degrees in international relations from California State University/Sacramento and in guidance and counseling from Truman State University, Kirksville, Missouri. His doctorate in mass communication is from the University of Iowa.

Farnsworth has received both the National and Midwest Regional CEO Leadership Awards from the American Association of Community College Trustees and in 1988 was named one of "America's Transformational Leaders in Higher Education" by the League for Innovation. He has served as a member of the American Association of Community Colleges Board of Directors and as member and chair of the Missouri State Humanities Council Board of Directors.

Farnsworth is one of the country's best-known advocates for internationalizing the culture and curriculum of the community college. His interest in international relations and comparative religion has taken him around the world. In addition to his teen years in Iran, he lived in England during his undergraduate years and spent the summer of 1994 as a Fulbright-Hays Fellow in Pakistan. In 1996, he was one of 13 educators awarded a Malone Fellowship for study in Saudi Arabia and Bahrain. Farnsworth spent the summer of 1998 with a group of faculty and students in the Ural region of South-Central Russia and in March of 2001 was one of a group of community college educators who traveled to Thailand to conduct workshops on the creation of a community college system. He was the 2002 recipient of the Werner Kubsch Award for Excellence in International Education, presented by Community Colleges for International Development.

Farnsworth's interest in distance education dates back nearly a decade, when as a college president he chose to model the use of online teaching and learning methods in his own instruction. For a decade he taught a world religions course in the classroom in the fall and online in the spring term. He now uses online formats for most of his teaching in the Community College Leadership program at UMSL.

Teresa Brawner Bevis is currently serving as an instructor for Crowder College in Missouri; she has taught Art History and Appreciation 101 as an online course since 2003. She previously taught art in a traditional classroom for Westark Community College in Arkansas.

Born in California to a family in the oil business, Bevis was raised on the Persian Gulf in Kuwait and attended the British primary schools that served the English-speaking residents of Kuwait City in the 1960s. During her childhood, she traveled in many areas of the Middle East, Asia, and Europe. After returning to the United States, she graduated from John Brown University with a bachelor's degree in art education and taught briefly before turning to business and pursuing a 15-year career as a fashion buyer in Philadelphia and New York. As the corporate head of the Women's Division for Urban Outfitters in Philadelphia, she used her art skills to design a line of clothing that sold internationally.

Returning to education in the 1990s, Bevis completed both a master's and doctorate in higher education administration at the University of Arkansas in Fayetteville, where she also served on staff as program coordinator for the university's 900 international students. Here Bevis developed global education programs for public schools and community organizations throughout northern Arkansas.

Bevis has published a number of articles in professional journals and periodicals related to international students and student programs and has produced English conversation workbooks and global education student handbooks that have been used in universities across the United States. She has also presented papers at professional educational conferences in Washington, DC, Denver, Philadelphia, Vancouver, Kansas City, San Antonio, and other locations.